AFTER ALL WE CAN DO

AFTER ALL WE CAN DO

EMBRACING HOPE, GRACE, AND JOY

DIETER F. UCHTDORF

DESERET
BOOK

SALT LAKE CITY, UTAH

Cover image: paul/Adobe Stock
Interior: simon/Adobe Stock; image on page viii courtesy of the author.
Book design © Deseret Book Company
Design: Garth Bruner

Visit us at DeseretBook.com

Library of Congress Cataloging-in-Publication Data
CIP on file
ISBN 978-1-63993-400-3

Printed in the United States of America
Publishers Printing, Salt Lake City, UT

10   9   8   7   6   5   4   3   2   1

CONTENTS

Dieter F. Uchtdorf at age eleven, shortly
after his family fled from East Germany.

INTRODUCTION

Toward the end of World War II, my father was drafted into the German army and sent to the western front, leaving my mother alone to care for our family. Though I was only three years old, I can still remember this time of fear and hunger. We lived in Czechoslovakia, and with every passing day, the war came nearer and the danger grew greater. Finally, during the cold winter of 1944, my mother decided to flee to East Germany, where her parents were living. My parents had decided earlier that this place offered the greatest hope for shelter and safety.

It was one of the coldest, harshest winters of World War II. My mother instructed us to take only warm clothes and food, but no other possessions. At this time, we were members of the Lutheran Church, not even aware that there was a restored Church of Jesus

Christ. Considering this, it is interesting that she took most of our family records and family pictures on our flight to the West.

As a four-year-old boy, I was so sad as we left behind our nice home with all my toys and a large balcony. How I loved this balcony and the view it provided, even though I once got my head stuck between two of its pillars—my ears kept me from getting back out again. Fortunately, there was my mother to help.

She bundled us up as we left our beloved home and somehow managed to get us on one of the last refugee trains heading west. Traveling during that time was dangerous. A freezing train, stopping over in refugee camps before heading out toward the West again, exhaustion, and fear were the continuous ingredients of this perilous flight. Everywhere we went, we saw distressed faces, and the ever-present hunger reminded us that we were in a war zone.

Along the way, the train stopped occasionally to get supplies. Often, kind people came to the stations and brought warm drinks and bread for the refugees. One night during one of these stops, my mother hurried out of the train to search for some food for her four children. When she returned to the platform where our train had stopped, to her great horror, the train and her children were gone!

She was weighed down with worry; desperate prayers filled her heart. She frantically searched the large and dark train station, urgently crisscrossing the numerous tracks while hoping against hope that the train had not already departed. Too many families were forever separated during these kinds of moments.

Perhaps I will never know all that went through my mother's heart and mind on that black night as she searched through a grim railroad station for her lost children. That she was terrified, I have no doubt. The physical stress of the effort to flee to the West and the emotional stress culminating in the apparent loss of all her children in a few minutes of time must have been overwhelming to her. I am certain it crossed her mind that if she did not find this train, she might never see her children again. But I know with certainty: her faith overcame her fear, and her hope overcame her despair. She was not a woman who would sit and bemoan tragedy. She moved. She put her faith and hope into action.

After a short period of terror and despair, she got on her feet and ran from track to track and from train to train until she finally found our train. It had been moved to a remote area of the station. There, at last, she found her children again.

I have often thought about that night and what my mother must have endured. If I could go back in time and sit by her side, I would ask her how she had managed to go on in the face of her fears. I would ask about faith and hope and how she had overcome despair in that moment.

My memories of those wartime days are of darkness, night, and cold.

My father eventually returned to us unharmed, but our future looked extremely bleak. We were living in the rubble of postwar Germany with a devastating feeling of hopelessness about our future. During this time of my childhood, I played in bombed-out houses and grew up with the ever-present consequences of a lost war and the awareness that my own country had inflicted terrible pain on many nations during the horrific World War II.

We were surrounded by chaos, fear, and uncertainties caused by war and political division. It was an anxious time for me, but it must have been terrifying for my beloved parents. My mother and father shared little about this burden with us four children. They bore the strain and suffering as best they could. The fear must have been oppressive, consuming their hours and dampening their hope.

This time of bleakness after World War II left its mark upon the world. It left its mark upon me. Back then, in the solitude of my loneliest hours, I often wondered, "Is there any hope left in the world?"

In the middle of this despair, my family learned about The Church of Jesus Christ of Latter-day Saints and the healing message of the restored gospel of Jesus Christ. This message made all the difference; it lifted us above our daily misery. While the world was drowning in cynicism, bitterness, hatred, and fear, the gospel filled me with hope. The gospel message transcended politics, history, grudges, grievances, and personal agendas. It gave divine answers to important questions we had during these difficult times.

The message was that God lived and cared about us, even in these hours of turmoil, confusion, and chaos. That He had actually appeared in our time to restore truth and light—to restore His gospel and His Church. We learned that He speaks to prophets again; that God is among us and is personally involved in our lives, actively guiding His children. Life was still thorny and the circumstances still horrible, but the gospel brought light, hope, grace, and joy into our lives. The plain and simple truths of the gospel warmed our hearts and enlightened our minds. They helped us look at ourselves and the world around us with different eyes and from an elevated viewpoint.

WELTSCHMERZ

In contrast to my mother's precarious situation desperately looking for her missing children or the palpable misery we experienced in World War II, sometimes the loss of hope is more abstract. But it can still affect us greatly. The ancient King Solomon was one of the most outwardly successful human beings in history. An msn.com poll listed Solomon as the fifth richest person to ever live. "According to the Bible, King Solomon ruled from 970 BC to 931 BC, and during this time he is said to have received 25 tons of gold for each of the 39 years of his reign, which would be worth billions of dollars in 2016. Along with impossible riches amassed from taxation and trade, the biblical ruler's personal fortune could have surpassed $2 trillion in today's money."[1] He seemed to have everything—money, power, adoration, honor. But after decades of self-indulgence and luxury, how did King Solomon sum up his life?

According to Ecclesiastes, he said, "All is vanity" (Ecclesiastes 1:2).

This man, who'd had it all, ended up disillusioned, pessimistic, and unhappy, despite everything he had going for him (see Ecclesiastes 2:17).

There is a word in German, *Weltschmerz*. Loosely defined, it means a sadness that comes from brooding about how the world is inferior to how we think it ought to be.

Perhaps there is a little *Weltschmerz* in all of us.

When silent sorrows creep into the corners of our lives. When sadness saturates our days and casts deep shadows over our nights. When tragedy and injustice enter the world around us, including in the lives of those we love. When we journey through our own personal and lonely path of misfortune, and pain darkens our stillness and breaches our tranquility. In times such as these, we might be tempted to agree with Solomon that life is vain and devoid of meaning.

The good news is that there is hope. That same hope that was available to my mother, my father, and even to Solomon is available to each of us through the "merits, and mercy, and grace of the Holy Messiah" (2 Nephi 2:8). There is a solution to the emptiness, vanity, and *Weltschmerz* of life. There is a solution to even the deepest hopelessness and discouragement you might feel. This hope is found in the transformative power of the gospel of Jesus Christ and in the Savior's redemptive power to heal us of our soul-sickness, offering us grace and leading us to enduring joy.

To help us receive the hope and grace that Jesus offers us, let us consider what scripture teaches us about these precious gifts, how we might choose to live in hope and grace, and how we can likewise offer them to others. All of this can work together "that [we] might have joy" (2 Nephi 2:25).

AFTER ALL WE CAN DO

Now we come to the language from the title of this book, "after all we can do" (2 Nephi 25:23). The prophet Nephi made an important contribution to our understanding of God's grace when he declared, "We labor diligently . . . to persuade our children, and also our brethren, to believe in Christ, and to be reconciled to God; for we know that it is *by grace that we are saved, after all we can do*" (2 Nephi 25:23; emphasis added).

However, I wonder how often we misinterpret the phrase "after all we can do." We must understand that "after" does not equal "because."

We are not saved "because" of all that we can do. We choose to receive Christ's grace; we don't earn it. Salvation cannot be bought with the currency of obedience; it is purchased by the blood of the Son of God (see Acts 20:28). Have any of us done *all* that we can do? Does God wait until we've expended every effort before He will intervene in our lives with His saving grace?

Many people feel discouraged because they constantly fall short. They know firsthand that "the spirit indeed is willing, but the flesh is weak" (Matthew 26:41; see also Romans 7:19). They raise their voices with Nephi in proclaiming, "My soul grieveth because of mine iniquities" (2 Nephi 4:17).

I am certain Nephi knew that the Savior's grace *allows* and *enables* us to overcome sin (see 2 Nephi 4:19–35; Alma 34:31). This is why Nephi labored so diligently to persuade his children and brethren "to believe in Christ, and to be reconciled to God" (2 Nephi 25:23). After all, *that is* what we can do! And *that is* our task in mortality!

All we can do is choose to receive grace as the Savior offers it to us. We can choose to receive hope, and ultimately to receive joy!

ABUNDANT JOY

Joy is the very purpose of God's plan for His children. It's what you were created for. Our Father in Heaven has not hidden the path to happiness. It is not a secret. It is available to all! It is promised to those who walk the path of discipleship, follow the teachings and example of the Savior, keep His commandments, and honor covenants they make with God. What a remarkable promise!

"I am come," Jesus declared, "that they might have life, and that they might have it more abundantly" (John 10:10). We achieve that abundant life not by focusing on our own needs or on our own achievements but by becoming true disciples of Jesus Christ—by following in His ways and engaging in His work. We find the abundant life by forgetting ourselves and engaging in the great cause of Christ.

And what is the cause of Christ? It is to believe in Him, love as He loved, and do as He did. Jesus "went about doing good" (Acts 10:38). He walked among the poor, the outcast, the sick, and the ashamed. He ministered to the powerless, the weak, and the friendless. He spent time with them; He spoke with them. "And he healed them all" (Matthew 12:15; see also 15:30).

Everywhere He went, the Savior taught the "good news" of the gospel. The word *gospel* has its roots in a Greek word that literally means "good news" (see Bible Dictionary, "Gospels"). He shared eternal truths that set people free spiritually as well as temporally.

Those who dedicate themselves to Christ's cause discover the truth of the Savior's promise: "Whosoever will lose his life for my sake shall find it" (Matthew 16:25).

Solomon was wrong, my dear brothers and sisters—life is not

"vanity." To the contrary, it can be full of purpose, meaning, and peace.

It is astonishing what we can learn when we look a little closer at our Heavenly Father's plan of salvation and exaltation, the plan of happiness, for His children. When we have times of feeling insignificant, cast off, and forgotten, we may be assured that God has not forgotten us—in fact, He offers to all His children something unimaginable: to become "heirs of God, and joint-heirs with Christ" (Romans 8:17; see also Doctrine and Covenants 84:38).

The healing hands of Jesus Christ reach out to all who seek Him. I have come to know without a doubt that believing and loving God and striving to follow Christ can change our hearts (see Ezekiel 36:26; Jeremiah 24:7), soften our pain, and fill our souls with "exceedingly great joy" (1 Nephi 8:12).

Wherever you live on this earth and whatever your life's situation may be, I testify to you that the gospel of Jesus Christ has the divine power to lift you to great heights from what appears at times to be an unbearable burden or weakness. The Lord knows your circumstances and your challenges. He said to Paul and to all of us, "My grace is sufficient for thee: for my strength is made perfect in weakness." And like Paul, we can answer: "Most gladly therefore will I rather glory in my infirmities, that the power of Christ may rest upon me" (2 Corinthians 12:9).

This means that we will live forever and have the potential to receive a fulness of joy (see 3 Nephi 28:10) and to "inherit thrones, kingdoms, principalities, and powers" (Doctrine and Covenants 132:19).

It is so humbling to know that this magnificent and supernal future is possible—not because of who we are but because of who God is.

Knowing this, how could we ever murmur or remain embittered? How could we ever keep our eyes on the ground when the King of kings invites us to take flight through hope and grace into an unimaginable future of divine happiness? (see Alma 28:12; Mormon 7:7).

Chapter 1

THE INFINITE POWER OF HOPE

Hope is one leg of a three-legged stool, together with faith and charity. There is a reason we find them together often in scripture.[1] These three stabilize our lives regardless of the rough or uneven surfaces we might encounter. The scriptures are clear and certain about the importance of hope. The Apostle Paul taught that the scriptures were written to the end that we "might have hope" (Romans 15:4).

Hope has the power to fill our lives with happiness (see Psalm 146:5). The absence of hope—when this desire of our heart is delayed—can, as the Proverb says, make "the heart sick" (Proverbs 13:12).

Hope is a gift of the Spirit (see Moroni 8:26). It is a hope that through the Atonement of Jesus Christ and the power of His Resurrection, we shall be raised unto life eternal, and this because of our faith in the Savior (see Moroni 7:41). This kind of hope is both a principle of promise as well as a commandment (see Colossians 1:21–23), and, as with all commandments, we have the responsibility to make it an active part of our lives and must overcome the temptation to lose hope. Hope in our Heavenly Father's merciful plan of happiness leads to peace, mercy, rejoicing, and gladness. The hope of salvation is like a protective helmet (see 1 Thessalonians 5:8); it is the foundation of our faith and an anchor to our souls.

Moroni in his solitude—even after having witnessed the complete destruction of his people—believed in hope. In the twilight of the Nephite nation, Moroni wrote that God has prepared a house for us, "even among the mansions of [the] Father." This is "a more excellent hope," without which we cannot receive an inheritance in the kingdom of God (Ether 12:32; see also Romans 8:24).

The scriptures say that there must be "an opposition in all things" (2 Nephi 2:11). So it is with faith, hope, and charity. Doubt, despair, and failure to care for others can lead us into temptation, which can cause us to forfeit choice and precious blessings.

The adversary uses despair to bind hearts and minds in suffocating darkness. Despair drains from us all that is vibrant and joyful and leaves behind the empty remnants of what life was meant to be. Despair kills ambition, advances sickness, pollutes the soul, and deadens the heart. Despair can seem like a staircase that leads only and forever downward.

Hope, on the other hand, is like the beam of sunlight rising up and above the horizon of our present circumstances. It pierces the darkness with a brilliant dawn. It encourages and inspires us to place our trust in the loving care of an eternal Heavenly Father, who has prepared a way for those who seek for eternal truth in a world of relativism, confusion, and fear. Indeed, love for and from our Father in Heaven is the root of all our hope.

WHY DOES GOD LOVE US?

God the Eternal Father did not give that first great commandment because He needs us to love Him. His power and glory are not diminished should we disregard, deny, or even defile His name. His influence and dominion extend through time and space independent of our acceptance, approval, or admiration.

No, God does not need us to love Him. But oh, how we need to love God!

For what we love determines what we seek.

What we seek determines what we think and do.

What we think and do determines who we are—and who we will become.

We are created in the image of our heavenly parents; we are

God's spirit children. Therefore, we have a vast capacity for love—it is part of our spiritual heritage. What and how we love not only defines us as individuals; it also defines us as a church. Love is the defining characteristic of a disciple of Christ.

Since the beginning of time, love has been the source of both the highest bliss and the heaviest burdens. At the heart of misery from the days of Adam until today, you will find the love of wrong things. And at the heart of joy, you will find the love of good things.

And the greatest of all good things is God.

Our Father in Heaven has given us, His children, much more than any mortal mind can comprehend. Under His direction the Great Jehovah created this wondrous world we live in. God the Father watches over us, fills our hearts with breathtaking joy, brightens our darkest hours with blessed peace, distills upon our minds precious truths, shepherds us through times of distress, rejoices when we rejoice, and answers our righteous petitions.

He offers to His children the promise of a glorious and infinite existence and has provided a way for us to progress in knowledge and glory until we receive a fulness of joy. He has promised us all that He has.

If all that is not enough reason to love our Heavenly Father, perhaps we can learn from the words of the Apostle John, who said, "We love him, because he first loved us" (1 John 4:19).

Think of the purest, most all-consuming love you can imagine.

Now multiply that love by an infinite amount—that is the measure of God's love for you. His "kindness shall not depart from thee" (Isaiah 54:10).

God does not look on the outward appearance (see 1 Samuel 16:7). I believe that He doesn't care one bit if we live in a castle or a cottage, if we are handsome or homely, if we are famous or forgotten. Though we are incomplete, God loves us completely. Though we are imperfect, He loves us perfectly. Though we may feel lost and without compass, God's love encompasses us completely.

He loves us because He is filled with an infinite measure of holy, pure, and indescribable love. We are important to God not because of our résumé but because we are His children. He loves every one of us, even those who are flawed, rejected, awkward, sorrowful, or broken. God's love is so great that He loves even the proud, the selfish, the arrogant, and the wicked.

What this means is that, regardless of our current state, there is hope for us. No matter our distress, no matter our sorrow, no matter our mistakes, our infinitely compassionate Heavenly Father desires that we draw near to Him so that He can draw near to us (see Doctrine and Covenants 88:63).

WHAT, THEN, IS HOPE?

The complexities of language offer several variations and intensities of the word *hope*. For example, a toddler may hope for a toy phone; an adolescent may hope for a phone call from a special friend; and an adult may simply hope that the phone will stop ringing altogether.

I wish to speak of the hope that transcends the trivial and centers on the Hope of Israel, the great hope of humankind, even our Redeemer, Jesus Christ.

Hope is not knowledge, but rather the abiding trust that the Lord will fulfill His promises to us. It is confidence that if we live according to God's laws and the words of His prophets now, we will receive desired blessings in the future—even "peace in this world, and eternal life in the world to come" (Doctrine and Covenants 59:23). It is believing and expecting that our prayers will be answered. It is manifest in confidence, optimism, enthusiasm, and patient perseverance.

In the language of the gospel, this hope is sure, unwavering, and active. The prophets of old speak of a "firm hope" (Alma 34:41) and a "lively hope" (1 Peter 1:3). It is a hope glorifying God through good works. With hope comes joy and happiness (see Psalm 146:5). With hope, we can "have patience, and bear . . . [our] afflictions" (Alma 34:41).

The things we hope *for* are often future events. If only we could look beyond the horizon of mortality into what awaits us beyond this life. Is it possible to imagine a more glorious future than the one prepared for us by our Heavenly Father? Because of the sacrifice of Jesus

Christ, we need not fear, for we will live forever, never to taste of death again (see Alma 11:45). Because of His infinite Atonement—His "merits, and mercy, and grace"—we can be cleansed of sin and stand pure and holy before the judgment bar (2 Nephi 2:6–10). The Savior is the Author of our Salvation.

And what kind of existence can we hope for? Those who come unto Christ, repent of their sins, and live in faith will reside forever in peace. Think of the worth of this eternal gift. Surrounded by those we love, we will know the meaning of ultimate joy as we progress in knowledge and in happiness. No matter how bleak the chapter of our lives may look today, because of the life and sacrifice of Jesus Christ, we may hope and be assured that the ending of the book of our lives will exceed our grandest expectations. "Eye hath not seen, nor ear heard, neither have entered into the heart of man, the things which God hath prepared for them that love him" (1 Corinthians 2:9).

The things we hope *in* sustain us during our daily walk. They uphold us through trials, temptations, and sorrow. Everyone has experienced discouragement and difficulty. Indeed, there are times when the darkness may seem unbearable. It is in these times that the divine principles of the restored gospel we hope *in* can uphold us and carry us until, once again, we walk in the light.

We hope in Jesus the Christ, in the goodness of God, in the manifestations of the Holy Spirit, in the knowledge that prayers are heard and answered. Because God has been faithful and kept His promises in the past, we can hope with confidence that God will keep His promises to us in the present and in the future. In times of distress, we can hold tightly to the hope that things will "work together for [our] good" as we follow the counsel of God's prophets (Doctrine and Covenants 90:24). This type of hope in God, His goodness, and His power refreshes us with courage during difficult challenges and gives strength to those who feel threatened by enclosing walls of fear, doubt, and despair.

A ROOM FILLED WITH DARKNESS

I'd like to tell you about a woman who grew up in a room filled with darkness—I'll call her Jane.

From the time Jane was three years old, she was repeatedly beaten, belittled, and abused. She was threatened and mocked. She awoke each morning not knowing if she would survive until the next day. The people who should have protected her were those who tortured her or allowed the abuse to continue.

In order to protect herself, Jane learned to stop feeling. She had no hope of rescue, so she hardened herself to the horror of her reality. There was no light in her world, so she became resigned to the darkness. With a numbness that can come only from constant and unrelenting contact with evil, she accepted the fact that any moment might be her last.

Then, at age eighteen, Jane discovered The Church of Jesus Christ of Latter-day Saints. The joy and hope of the restored gospel penetrated her heart, and she accepted the invitation to be baptized. For the first time, light entered her life, and she saw a bright path before her. She left the darkness of her world and decided to attend school a great distance away from her abuser. At last she felt liberated from an environment of darkness and evil—free to enjoy the Savior's sweet peace and miraculous healing.

However, years later, after her abuser had died, Jane was again troubled by the horrible events of her youth. Profound sadness and anger threatened to destroy the wonderful light she had found in the gospel. She realized that if she allowed that darkness to consume her, her tormentor would have a final victory.

She sought counseling and medical help and began to realize that, for her, the best path for healing was to understand and accept that darkness exists—but not to dwell there. For, as she now knew, light also exists—and that is where she chose to dwell.

Given her difficult past, Jane could easily have become vindictive, venomous, or violent. But she didn't. She resisted the path of adding more pain to the world, refusing to lash out in anger, hurt, or cynicism. Instead, she held fast to the hope that with God's help she could be healed. She chose to radiate light and devote her life to helping others. This decision enabled her to leave the past behind and to step into a glorious, bright future.

She became a schoolteacher, and today, decades later, her love has influenced the lives of hundreds of children, helping them to know that they have worth, that they are important. She has become a tireless defender of the weak, the victimized, and the discouraged. She builds, strengthens, and inspires everyone around her.

Jane learned that healing comes when we move away from the darkness and walk toward the hope of a brighter light. It was in the practical application of faith, hope, and charity that she not only transformed her own life but forever blessed the lives of many, many others.

LIGHT CLEAVETH UNTO LIGHT

You may at times feel darkness encroaching upon you. You may feel burdened by worry, fear, or doubt. To you and to all of us, I repeat a wonderful and certain truth: God's light is real. It is available to all! It gives life to all things (see Doctrine and Covenants 88:11–13). It has the power to soften the sting of the deepest wound. It can be a healing balm for the loneliness and sickness of our souls. In the furrows of despair, it can plant the seeds of a brighter hope. It can enlighten the deepest valleys of sorrow. It can illuminate the path before us and lead us through the darkest night into the promise of a new dawn.

This is "the Spirit of Jesus Christ," which gives "light to every man that cometh into the world" (Doctrine and Covenants 84:45–46).

Nevertheless, spiritual light rarely comes to those who merely sit in darkness waiting for someone to flip a switch. It takes an act of faith to open our eyes to the Light of Christ. Spiritual light cannot be discerned by carnal eyes. Jesus Christ Himself taught, "I am the light which shineth in darkness, and the darkness comprehendeth it not" (Doctrine and Covenants 6:21). For "the natural man receiveth not the things of the Spirit of God: for they are foolishness unto him: neither can he know them, because they are spiritually discerned" (1 Corinthians 2:14).

So how do we open our eyes to the hope of God's light?

First, start where you are.

Isn't it wonderful to know that we don't have to be perfect to experience the blessings and gifts of our Heavenly Father? We don't have to wait to cross the finish line to receive God's blessings. In fact, the heavens begin to part and the blessings of heaven begin to distill upon us with the very first steps we take toward the light.

The perfect place to begin is exactly where you are right now. It doesn't matter how unqualified you may think you are or how far behind others you may feel. The very moment you begin to seek your Heavenly Father, the hope of His light will begin to awaken, enliven, and ennoble your soul (see Alma 34:31). The darkness may not dissipate all at once, but as surely as night always gives way to dawn, the light will come.

Second, turn your heart toward the Lord.

Lift up your soul in prayer and explain to your Heavenly Father what you are feeling. Acknowledge your shortcomings. Pour out your heart and express your gratitude. Let Him know of the trials you are facing. Plead with Him in Christ's name for strength and support. Ask that your ears may be opened, that you may hear His voice. Ask that your eyes may be opened, that you may see His light.

Third, walk in the light.

Your Heavenly Father knows that you will make mistakes. He knows that you will stumble—perhaps many times. This saddens Him, but He loves you. He does not wish to break your spirit. On the contrary, He desires that you rise up and become the person you were designed to be.

To that end, He sent His Son to this earth to illuminate the way and show us how to safely cross the stumbling blocks placed in our path. He has given us the gospel, which teaches the way of the disciple. It teaches us the things we must know, do, and be to walk in His light, following in the footsteps of His Beloved Son, our Savior.

Yes, we will make mistakes.

Yes, we will falter.

But as we seek to increase our love for God and strive to love our neighbor, the light of the gospel will surround and uplift us. The darkness will surely fade, because it cannot exist in the presence of light. As we draw near to God, He will draw near to us (see James 4:8; Doctrine and Covenants 88:63). And day by day, the hope of

God's light will grow within us, "brighter and brighter until the perfect day" (Doctrine and Covenants 50:24).

To all who feel they walk in darkness, I invite you to rely on this certain promise spoken by the Savior of humankind: "I am the light of the world: he that followeth me shall not walk in darkness, but shall have the light of life" (John 8:12).

HOPE LEADS TO GOOD WORKS

We learn to cultivate hope the same way we learn to walk, one step at a time. As we study the scriptures, speak with our Heavenly Father daily, and commit to keep the commandments of God, we attain hope (see Romans 15:14). We grow in our ability to "abound in hope, through the power of the Holy Ghost" (Romans 15:13), as we more perfectly live the gospel.

There may be times when we must make a courageous decision to hope even when everything around us contradicts this hope. Like Father Abraham, we will "against hope [believe] in hope" (Romans 4:18). Or, as one writer expressed, "in the depth of winter, [we find] within [us] an invincible summer."[2]

Faith, hope, and charity complement each other, and as one increases, the others grow as well. Hope comes of faith (see Ether 12:4), for without faith, there *is* no hope (see Moroni 7:42). In like manner faith comes of hope, for faith is "the substance of things hoped for" (Hebrews 11:1).

Hope is critical to both faith and charity. When disobedience, disappointment, and procrastination erode faith, hope is there to uphold our faith. When frustration and impatience challenge charity, hope braces our resolve and urges us to care for our neighbors even without expectation of reward. The brighter our hope, the greater our faith. The stronger our hope, the purer our charity.

The things we hope *for* lead us to faith, while the things we hope *in* lead us to charity. The three qualities—faith, hope, and charity (see Moroni 10:20)—working together, grounded on the truth and light of the restored gospel of Jesus Christ, lead us to abound in good works (see Alma 7:24).

HOPE FROM PERSONAL EXPERIENCE

Each time a hope is fulfilled, it creates confidence and leads to greater hope. I can think of many instances in my life when I learned firsthand the power of hope. I well remember the days in my childhood encompassed by the horrors and despair of a world war, the lack of educational opportunities, life-threatening health issues during youth, and the challenging and discouraging economic experiences as a refugee. The example of my parents, even in the worst of times, to move forward and put faith and hope into action, rather than only worrying or wishfully thinking, sustained our family and me and gave us confidence that present circumstances would give way to future blessings.

True faith in Jesus Christ will evidence itself in our actions. Faith is not manifest merely through those things that we verbally declare, but rather that which we do. We need to put our faith into practice with constancy and solidity, with an endurance like that of the Apostles in the old days who also had to struggle with their faith. After the Resurrection of Christ, even Thomas had his struggles. But with endurance, patience, and hope, he managed to strengthen his faith and live up to the calling and the authority that he had been given.

When we put our faith into action, we can radiate the hope, confidence, optimism, excitement, and patient endurance that will help draw others unto Christ. If we will have hope, if we will seek for the help that the gospel can bring us, then we will also be able to cope with our trials.

Hope sustains us through despair. Hope teaches that there is reason to rejoice even when all seems dark around us.

With Jeremiah I proclaim, "Blessed is the man . . . whose hope the Lord is" (Jeremiah 17:7).

With Joel I testify, "The Lord [is] the hope of his people, and the strength of the children of Israel" (Joel 3:16).

With Nephi I declare, "Press forward with a steadfastness in Christ, having a perfect brightness of hope, and a love of God and of all men. Wherefore, if ye shall press forward, feasting upon the word of Christ, and endure to the end, behold, thus saith the Father: Ye shall have eternal life" (2 Nephi 31:20).

This is the quality of hope we must cherish and develop. Such a mature hope comes in and through our Savior Jesus Christ, for "every man that hath this hope in him purifieth himself, even as [the Savior] is pure" (1 John 3:3).

The Lord has given us a reassuring message of hope: "Fear not, little flock" (Doctrine and Covenants 6:34). God will wait with "open arms to receive" those who give away their sins and continue in faith, hope, and charity (Mormon 6:17).

To all who suffer—to all who feel discouraged, worried, or lonely—I say with love and deep concern for you, never give up. Never allow despair to overcome your spirit. Embrace and rely upon the Hope of Israel, for the love of the Son of God pierces all darkness, softens all sorrow, and gladdens every heart.

I know from personal experience that it is the gospel of Jesus Christ and our covenants with our Heavenly Father that strengthen faith, offer a bright hope, and lead us to charity, or the pure love of Christ, and His incomparable gift of grace.

COME TO THE LIGHT

Of course, from time to time our lives may seem to be touched by, or even wrapped in, darkness. Sometimes the night that surrounds us will appear oppressive, disheartening, and frightening.

My heart grieves for the many sorrows you may face throughout this life, for the painful loneliness and wearisome fears you may be experiencing.

Nevertheless, I bear witness that our living hope is in Christ Jesus! He is the true, pure, and powerful entrance to divine enlightenment. I testify that with Christ, darkness cannot succeed. Darkness will not gain victory over the light of Christ. I bear witness that darkness cannot stand before the brilliant light of the Son of the living God!

I invite you to open your heart to Him. Seek Him through study, prayer, and applying His teachings. Gather in His Church, even The Church of Jesus Christ of Latter-day Saints. Learn of Him and of His gospel, participate actively, help each other, and joyfully serve our God.

Even after the darkest night, the Savior of the world will lead you to a gradual, sweet, and bright dawn that will assuredly rise within you.

As you walk toward the hope of God's light, you will discover the compassion, love, and goodness of a loving Heavenly Father, "in [whom there] is no darkness at all" (1 John 1:5).

Chapter 2

THE GIFT OF GRACE

Once I did a Google search, asking: "What day most changed the course of history?"

The responses ranged from surprising and strange to insightful and thought-provoking. Among them were the day when a prehistoric asteroid struck the Yucatán Peninsula; or when in 1440, Johannes Gutenberg finished his printing press; and, of course, the day in 1903 when the Wright brothers showed the world that man really can fly. If the same question were asked of you, what would you say?

In my mind the answer is clear.

To find the most important day in history, we must go back to that evening almost 2,000 years ago in the Garden of Gethsemane when Jesus Christ knelt in intense prayer and offered Himself as a ransom for our sins. It was during this great and infinite sacrifice of unparalleled suffering in both body and spirit that Jesus Christ, even God, bled at every pore. Out of perfect love, He gave all that we might receive all. His supernal sacrifice, difficult to comprehend, to be felt only with all our heart and mind, reminds us of the universal debt of gratitude we owe Christ for His divine gift.

Later that night, Jesus was brought before religious and political authorities who mocked Him, beat Him, and sentenced Him to a shameful death. He hung in agony upon the cross until, finally, "it [was] finished" (John 19:30). His lifeless body was laid in a borrowed tomb. And then, on the morning of the third day, Jesus Christ, the Son of Almighty God, emerged from the tomb as a glorious, resurrected being of splendor, light, and majesty.

Yes, there are many events throughout history that have profoundly affected the destiny of nations and peoples. But combine them all, and they cannot begin to compare to the importance of what happened on that first Easter morning.

What is it that makes the infinite sacrifice and the Resurrection of Jesus Christ the most important event in history—more influential than world wars, cataclysmic disasters, and life-changing scientific discoveries?

The answer lies in two great, insurmountable challenges that every one of us faces.

First, we all die. No matter how young, beautiful, healthy, or cautious you are, someday your body will become lifeless. Friends and family will mourn you. But they cannot bring you back.

Nevertheless, because of Jesus Christ, your death will be temporary. Your spirit one day will reunite with your body. This resurrected body will not be subject to death (see Alma 11:45), and you will live in the eternities, free from pain and physical suffering (see Revelation 21:4).

This will happen because of Jesus the Christ, who laid down His life and took it up again.

He did this for all who believe in Him.

He did this for all who do not believe in Him.

He did this even for those who mock, revile, and curse His name (see 1 Corinthians 15:21–23).

Second, we have all sinned.[1] Our sins would forever keep us from living with God, because "no unclean thing can enter into his kingdom" (3 Nephi 27:19).

As a result, every man, woman, and child was shut out of His presence—that is, until Jesus Christ, the Lamb without spot, offered His life as a ransom for our sins. Because Jesus owed no debt to justice, He could pay our debt and meet the demands of justice for every soul. And that includes you and me.

Jesus Christ paid the price for our sins.

All of them.

On that most important day in history, Jesus the Christ opened the gates of death and cast aside the barriers that prevented us from passing into the holy and hallowed halls of everlasting life. Because of our Lord and Savior, you and I are granted a most precious and priceless gift—regardless of our past, we can repent and follow the path that leads to celestial light and glory, surrounded by the faithful children of Heavenly Father.

Because of Jesus Christ, we will rise from the despair of death and embrace those we love, shedding tears of overwhelming joy and overflowing gratitude. Because of Jesus Christ, we will exist as eternal beings, worlds without end.

Because of Jesus the Christ, our sins can not only be erased, they can be forgotten.

We can become purified and exalted.

Holy.

Because of our beloved Savior, we can forever drink from the fountain of water that springs up into eternal life (see John 4:14). We can dwell forever in the mansions of our eternal King, in unimaginable glory and perfect happiness.

SALVATION AMONG US

Because of God's perfect love for us and the eternal sacrifice of Jesus Christ, our sins—both great and small—can be blotted out and remembered no more. The words of Doctrine and Covenants 58:42 are some of the most inspiring and encouraging in scripture:

"He who has repented of his sins, the same is forgiven, and I, the Lord, remember them no more." What joy this gives me to know that if I continue to repent, in that future day when I shall fall on my knees before my Savior and Redeemer, He will lift me up and embrace me. My sins will not only be forgiven, they will not even be remembered. We can stand before Him pure, worthy, and sanctified.

My heart overflows with gratitude for my Heavenly Father. I realize that He has not doomed His children to stumble through mortality without hope for a bright and eternal future. He has provided instructions that reveal the way back to Him. And at the center of it all is *His Beloved Son, Jesus Christ,* and His sacrifice for us (see Luke 9:35; Joseph Smith—History 1:17).

The Savior's infinite Atonement completely changes the way we may view our transgressions and imperfections. Instead of dwelling on them and feeling irredeemable or hopeless, we can learn from them and feel hopeful. Though the memory of our past sins might tear at us, the pain associated with those sins can disappear, and like Alma, we can be "filled with joy" through the Savior's mercy (Alma 36:17–20). The cleansing gift of repentance allows us to leave our sins behind and emerge "a new creature" (2 Corinthians 5:17).

Because of Jesus Christ, our failures do not have to define us. They can refine us.

Like a musician rehearsing scales, we can see our missteps, flaws, and sins as opportunities for greater self-awareness, deeper and more honest love for others, and refinement through repentance.

If we repent, mistakes do not disqualify us. They are part of our progress.

We are all infants compared to the beings of glory and grandeur we are designed to become. No mortal being advances from crawling to walking to running without frequent stumbles, bumps, and bruises. That is how we learn.

If we earnestly keep practicing, always striving to keep God's commandments, and committing our efforts to repenting, enduring, and applying what we learn, line upon line, we will gather light into our souls (see Doctrine and Covenants 50:24). And though we may not fully comprehend our full potential now, "we know that, when [the Savior] shall appear," we will see His countenance in us and "shall see him as he is" (1 John 3:2).

What a glorious promise!

Yes, the world is in turmoil. And yes, we have weaknesses. But we do not need to hang our heads in despair, because we can trust God, we can trust His Son, Jesus Christ, and we can accept the gift of the Spirit to guide us on this path toward a life filled with joy and divine happiness (see Mormon 7:7).

The good news is that Jesus Christ has made the perfect Atonement for all, redeeming all from the grave and rewarding each individual according to his or her works. The Atonement of Jesus Christ is the healing power that can bring hope and peace back into all of our lives.

Whatever our challenges in life may be, our burdens may become light if we not only believe in Christ but also in His ability and His power to cleanse and console our lives.

That day nearly 2,000 years ago was indeed the most long-awaited and glorious event in the history of the world.

It is the day that changed everything.

On that day, my life changed.

Your life changed.

The destiny of all God's children changed.

On that blessed day, the Savior of all, who had taken upon Himself the chains of sin and death that held us captive, burst those chains and set us free.

Because of the sacrifice of our beloved Redeemer, death has no sting, the grave has no victory, Satan has no lasting power, and we are "begotten . . . again unto a lively hope by the resurrection of Jesus Christ" (1 Peter 1:3).

Truly, the Apostle Paul was correct when he said we can "comfort one another with these words" (1 Thessalonians 4:18).

GOD'S GRACE AS A GIFT

We often speak of the Savior's Atonement—and rightly so! In Jacob's words, "Why not speak of the atonement of Christ, and attain to a perfect knowledge of him?" (Jacob 4:12). But as "we talk of Christ, . . . rejoice in Christ, . . . preach of Christ, [and] prophesy of Christ" at every opportunity, we must never lose our sense of awe and profound gratitude for the eternal sacrifice of the Son of God (2 Nephi 25:26). The Savior's Atonement cannot become common-place in our teaching, in our conversation, or in our hearts. It is sacred and holy, for it was through this "great and last sacrifice" that Jesus the Christ brought "salvation to all those who shall believe on his name" (Alma 34:10, 15).

I marvel to think that the Son of God would condescend to save us, as imperfect, impure, mistake-prone, and ungrateful as we often are. I have tried to understand the Savior's Atonement with my finite mind, and the only explanation I can come up with is this: God loves us deeply, perfectly, and everlastingly. I cannot even begin to estimate "the breadth, and length, and depth, and height . . . [of] the love of Christ" (Ephesians 3:18–19).

A powerful expression of that love is what the scriptures often call the *grace of God*—the divine assistance and endowment of strength by which we grow from the flawed and limited beings we are now into exalted beings of "truth and light, until [we are] glorified in truth and [know] all things" (Doctrine and Covenants 93:28).

It is a most wondrous thing, this grace of God. Yet it is often misunderstood—we do not fully understand the blessings our Father has prepared for us (see Doctrine and Covenants 78:17). Even so, we should know about God's grace if we intend to inherit what has been prepared for us in His eternal kingdom. To that end, let's consider first how grace *unlocks the gates of heaven* and, second, how it *opens the windows of heaven.*

Unlocking the Gates of Heaven

Because we have all "sinned, and come short of the glory of God" (Romans 3:23) and because "there cannot any unclean thing enter into the kingdom of God" (1 Nephi 15:34), every one of us is unworthy to return to God's presence (see also 1 Nephi 10:21; Moses 6:57).

Even if we were to serve God with our whole souls, it would not be enough, for we would still be "unprofitable servants," as King Benjamin taught (Mosiah 2:21). We cannot earn our way into heaven; the demands of justice stand as a barrier, which we are powerless to overcome on our own.

But all is not lost.

The grace of God is our great and everlasting hope.

Through the sacrifice of Jesus Christ, the plan of mercy appeases the demands of justice "and [brings] about means unto men that they may have faith unto repentance" (Alma 34:15). Our sins, though they may be as scarlet, can become white as snow (see Isaiah 1:18). Because our beloved Savior "gave himself a ransom for all"

(1 Timothy 2:6), an entrance into His everlasting kingdom is provided unto us (see 2 Peter 1:11).

The gate is unlocked!

But the grace of God does not merely restore us to our previous innocent state. If salvation means only erasing our mistakes and sins, then salvation—as wonderful as it is—does not fulfill the Father's aspirations for us. His aim is much higher: He wants His sons and daughters to become like Him. With the gift of God's grace, the path of discipleship does not lead backward; it leads upward.

It leads to heights we can scarcely comprehend! It leads to exaltation in the celestial kingdom of our Heavenly Father, where we, surrounded by our loved ones, receive "of his fulness, and of his glory" (Doctrine and Covenants 76:56). All things are ours, and we are Christ's (see Doctrine and Covenants 76:59). Indeed, all that the Father hath shall be given unto us (see Doctrine and Covenants 84:38).

To inherit this glory, we need more than an unlocked gate; we must enter through this gate with a heart's desire to be changed—a change so dramatic that the scriptures describe it as being "born again; yea, born of God, changed from [our worldly] and fallen state, to a state of righteousness, being redeemed of God, becoming his sons and daughters" (Mosiah 27:25).

Opening the Windows of Heaven

Another element of God's grace is the opening of the windows of heaven, through which God pours out blessings of power and strength, enabling us to achieve things that otherwise would be far beyond our reach. It is by God's amazing grace that His children can overcome the undercurrents and quicksands of the deceiver, rise above sin, and "be perfect[ed] in Christ" (Moroni 10:32).

Though we all have weaknesses, we can overcome them through His grace. Indeed it is by the grace of God that, if we humble ourselves and have faith, weak things can become strong (see Ether 12:27).

Throughout our lives, God's grace bestows temporal blessings and spiritual gifts that magnify our abilities and enrich our lives. His grace refines us. His grace helps us become our best selves.

HOW DO WE RECEIVE GRACE?

In the Bible we read of Christ's visit to the home of Simon the Pharisee. Outwardly, Simon seemed to be a good and upright man. He regularly checked off his to-do list of religious obligations: he kept the law, paid his tithing, observed the Sabbath, prayed daily, and went to the synagogue.

But while Jesus was with Simon, a woman approached, washed the Savior's feet with her tears, and anointed His feet with fine oil. Simon was not pleased with this display of worship, for he knew that this woman was a sinner. Simon thought that if Jesus didn't know this, He must not be a prophet or He would not have let the woman touch Him.

Perceiving his thoughts, Jesus turned to Simon and asked a question. "There was a certain creditor which had two debtors: . . . one owed five hundred pence, . . . the other fifty.

"And when they [both] had nothing to pay, he frankly forgave them both. Tell me therefore, which of them will love him most?"

Simon answered that it was the one who was forgiven the most.

Then Jesus taught a profound lesson: "Seest thou this woman? . . . Her sins, which are many, are forgiven; *for she loved much:* but to whom little is forgiven, the same loveth little" (Luke 7:36–50); emphasis added).

Which of these two people are we most like?

Are we like Simon? Are we confident and comfortable in our good deeds, trusting in our own righteousness? Are we perhaps a little impatient with those who are not living up to our standards? Are we on autopilot, going through the motions, attending our meetings, yawning through Sunday School class, and perhaps checking our cell phones during sacrament service?

Or are we like this woman, who thought she was completely and hopelessly lost because of sin? She was the one who "loved much" (Luke 7:47).

Do we *love much*?

Do we understand our indebtedness to Heavenly Father and plead with all our souls for the grace of God?

Christ's parable of the Pharisee and the tax collector also illustrates this point clearly. These two men went into the temple to pray. The Pharisee prayed: "God, I thank thee, that I am not as other men are, extortioners, unjust, adulterers, or even as this publican. I fast twice in the week, I give tithes of all that I possess."

The other man, a hated publican, stood "afar off, [and] would not lift up so much as his eyes unto heaven, but smote upon his breast, saying, God be merciful to me a sinner."

And Jesus said, "I tell you, this man went down to his house justified rather than the other" (Luke 18:9–14).

In truth, we "all have sinned, and come short of the glory of God" (Romans 3:23). We are all in need of mercy. In that last day when we are called to the judgment bar of God, do we not hope that our many imperfections will be forgiven? Do we not yearn to feel the Savior's embrace?

When we kneel to pray, is it to replay the greatest hits of our own righteousness, or is it to confess our faults, plead for God's mercy, and shed tears of gratitude for the amazing plan of redemption? Salvation cannot be bought with the currency of obedience; it is purchased by the blood of the Son of God (see Acts 20:28). Thinking that we can trade our good works for salvation is like buying a plane ticket and then supposing we own the airline. Or thinking that after paying rent for our home, we now hold title to the entire planet earth.

WHY THEN OBEY?

If grace is a gift of God, why then is obedience to God's commandments so important? Why bother with God's commandments—or repentance, for that matter? Why not just admit we're sinful and let God save us? This is what some might call "easy grace."

Or, to put the question in Paul's words, "Shall we continue in sin, that grace may abound?" Paul's answer is simple and clear: "God forbid" (Romans 6:1–2).

So why then do we obey? We obey the commandments of God out of love for Him!

Trying to understand God's gift of grace with all our heart and mind gives us all the more reason to love and obey our Heavenly Father with meekness and gratitude. As we walk the path of discipleship, it refines us, it improves us, it helps us to become more like Him, and it leads us back to His presence. "The Spirit of the Lord [our God]" brings about such "a mighty change in us . . . that we have no more disposition to do evil, but to do good continually" (Mosiah 5:2).

Therefore, our obedience to God's commandments comes as a natural outgrowth of our endless love and gratitude for the goodness of God. This form of genuine love and gratitude will miraculously merge our works with God's grace. Virtue will garnish our thoughts unceasingly, and our "confidence [will] wax strong in the presence of God" (Doctrine and Covenants 121:45).

Living the gospel faithfully is not a burden. It is a joyful rehearsal—a preparation for inheriting the grand glory of the eternities. We seek to obey our Heavenly Father because our spirits will become more attuned to spiritual things. Vistas are opened that we never knew existed. Enlightenment and understanding come to us when we do the will of the Father (see John 7:17).

Grace is a gift of God, and our desire to be obedient to each of God's commandments is the reaching out of our mortal hand to receive this sacred gift from our Heavenly Father.

NEPHI AND ALL WE CAN DO

As we discussed in the introduction, toward the end of 2 Nephi, we encounter this verse: "We labor diligently . . . to persuade our children, and also our brethren, to believe in Christ, and to be reconciled to God; for we know that it is *by grace that we are saved, after all we can do*" (2 Nephi 25:23; emphasis added). *Reconcile* is the word that Jacob and Nephi use when talking about the Atonement of Jesus Christ (see 2 Nephi 10:24; 33:9; Jacob 4:11). We find this same language in the New Testament (see Romans 5:10; 2 Corinthians 5:18–19; Colossians 1:20–21).

Sometimes we quickly read this single verse and forget everything else Nephi, Jacob, and Lehi have taught us about grace. Remember, "after all we can do" does not mean "because of all we have done."

Although the scriptural phrasing might be unfamiliar to us and perhaps is misunderstood in the twenty-first century, it was language familiar to Joseph Smith as he translated the Book of Mormon. In the language of his time, "after all we can do" more closely meant apart from what we can do or in spite of all we can do.[2] As one scholar explained, "Another acceptable paraphrase of the sense of the verse might read, 'We are still saved by grace, after all is said and done.'"[3]

We are not saved "because" of all that we can do. President M. Russell Ballard phrased it as, "It is through His grace that we are saved *even after* all we can do." He taught, "As we embrace His teachings, we give up all of our sins, we repent, we do all that is in our power to do to come unto Him in a true spirit of disciple-ship, knowing perfectly well that it is through His grace that we are saved, *even after* all that we can do. And as we give ourselves to Christ, fully and completely, we find safety, peace, joy and security in Him."[4]

With Nephi, "we talk of Christ, we rejoice in Christ, we preach of Christ, we prophesy of Christ." And we "believe in Christ" (2 Nephi 25:26, 29). He is the one who offers us His grace and offers us salvation. In Alma's words, "all we can do" is enter the covenant and repent (Alma 24:11). All we can do is receive what Christ has offered us. We rely on hope and grace that stems from Christ. If we accept His offering, we will "repent and harden not [our] hearts, [and] immediately . . . the great plan of redemption [will] be brought about" for us (Alma 34:31).

GRACE IS AVAILABLE TO ALL

We acknowledge that "all have sinned, and come short of the glory of God" (Romans 3:23), but we also declare with firmness that repentance and forgiveness can be as real as sin. The Atonement of Jesus Christ causes each person to be accountable for his or her individual sins. We will overcome the consequences of individual sin by claiming the blessings and benefits of the Atonement.

As Elder Quentin L. Cook instructed, "None can return to God by his or her own good works alone; we all need the benefit of the Savior's sacrifice. All have sinned, and it is only through the Atonement of Jesus Christ that we can obtain mercy and live with God."[5] Likewise King Benjamin testified, "For salvation cometh to none . . . except it be through repentance and faith on the Lord Jesus Christ" (Mosiah 3:12).

It is not repentance per se that saves mankind. It is the blood of Jesus Christ that saves us. It is not by our sincere and honest change of behavior alone that we are saved, but "by grace that we are saved, after all we can do" (2 Nephi 25:23). When King Lamoni's people were converted, they knew that it was "all [they] could do to repent" and rely on Christ (Alma 24:11). True repentance is the condition required so that God's forgiveness can come into our lives. As President Russell M. Nelson has taught, true repentance "allow[s] the Savior to transform us into the best version of ourselves."[6]

When I think of what the Savior did for us, I want to lift up my voice and shout praises to the Most High God and His Son, Jesus Christ!

The gates of heaven are unlocked!

The windows of heaven are opened!

Today and forevermore, God's grace is available to all whose hearts are broken and whose spirits are contrite (see 3 Nephi 9:19–20). Jesus Christ has cleared the way for us to ascend to heights incomprehensible to mortal minds (see 1 Corinthians 2:9). Let us consider what Jesus taught us about our dependence on God and the importance of our relationship with Him.

Chapter 3

PRODIGALS ALL

I t has been called by some the greatest short story ever told. Found in Luke 15, the parable is one of three (the lost sheep, the lost coin, and the lost son) that illustrate the value of lost things and the celebration that occurs when that which was lost is found. Since the parable of the prodigal son has been translated into thousands of languages across the world, it is quite possible that during the past two millennia, the sun has not set without the story being referenced somewhere in the world.

It was told by Jesus Christ, our Savior and Redeemer, who came to earth "to save that which was lost" (Luke 19:10). He begins with these simple words: "A certain man had two sons" (Luke 15:11).

Immediately we learn of a heartbreaking conflict. One son tells his father he is through with life at home. This son was probably young. He was unmarried, which may be an indication of his youth, but not so young that he wasn't able to demand his inheritance and leave home once he had obtained it. He wants his freedom. He wants to leave behind the culture and teachings of his parents. He asks for his share of the inheritance—now.[1]

Can you imagine what the father felt when he heard this? When he realized that what his son wanted more than anything else was to leave the family and perhaps never return?

THE GREAT ADVENTURE

The son must have felt a thrill of adventure and excitement. At long last, he was on his own. Free from the principles and rules of the culture of his youth, he could finally make his own choices without being influenced by his parents. No more guilt. He could bask in the acceptance of a like-minded community and live life on his own terms.

Arriving in a faraway country, he quickly made new friends and began living the life he had always dreamed of. He must have been a favorite of many, for he spent money freely. His new friends—beneficiaries of his prodigality—did not judge him. They celebrated, applauded, and championed his choices (see Luke 15:13). Had there been social media in that time, surely he would have filled pages with animated photos of laughing friends: #Livingmybestlife! #Neverhappier! #Shouldhavedonethislongago!

But the party did not last—it rarely does. Two things happened: first, he ran out of money, and second, a famine swept through the land (see Luke 15:14). As the problems worsened, he panicked. The once unstoppable, jubilant high roller now could not afford a single meal, let alone a place to stay. How would he survive? He had been generous to his friends—would they help him now? I can see him asking for a little support—just for now—until he got back on his feet.

The scriptures tell us, "No man gave unto him" (Luke 15:16).

Desperate to remain alive, he found a local farmer who hired him to feed swine. To the Jews, pigs were considered "unclean" (see Deuteronomy 14:8) and were offensive. Practicing Jews would not have raised swine, which indicates the overseer was a Gentile. It could also suggest how far the young son had traveled to be away from practicing Jews. Extremely hungry now, abandoned and alone, the young man must have wondered how things could have gone so terribly, dreadfully wrong.

It wasn't just an empty stomach that troubled him. It was an empty soul. He had been so sure that giving in to his worldly desires would make him happy, that moral laws were obstacles to that happiness. Now he knew better. And oh, what a price he had to pay for that knowledge![2]

As the physical and spiritual hunger grew, his thoughts returned to his father. Would he help him after all that had happened? Even the humblest of his father's servants had food to eat and shelter from the storms.

But return to his father?

Never.

Confess to his village that he had squandered his inheritance? Impossible.

Face the neighbors who surely had warned him that he was disgracing his family and breaking his parents' hearts? Return to his old friends after boasting of how he was breaking free?

Unbearable.

But the hunger, loneliness, and remorse simply wouldn't go away—until "he came to himself" (Luke 15:17).

He knew what he needed to do.

THE RETURN

Now let us go back to the father, the brokenhearted master of the house. How many hundreds, perhaps thousands, of hours had he spent worrying about his son? How many times had he looked down the very road his son had taken and relived the penetrating loss he had felt as his son walked away? How many prayers had he offered in the deep of night, pleading with God that his son would be safe, that he would discover truth, that he would return?

And then one day, the father looks out on that lonely road—*the road that leads home*—and sees a distant figure walking toward him.

Is it possible?

Though the individual is a great way off, the father knows in an instant it is his son.

He runs to him, throws his arms around him, and kisses him (see Luke 15:20).

"Father," the son cries out, in words he must have rehearsed a thousand times, "I have sinned against both heaven and you. I am no longer worthy to be called your son. All I ask is that you take me in as a hired servant" (see Luke 15:18–19, 21).

But the father scarcely lets him finish. Tears in his eyes, he commands his servants: "Bring the finest robe in the house and place it on my son's shoulders. Put a ring on his finger and sandals on his feet. Make a feast to celebrate. My son has returned!" (see Luke 15:22–24).

THE CELEBRATION

For many years I had a painting in my office by the German artist Richard Burde. Harriet and I love this painting. It depicts one tender scene from the Savior's parable in a deeper perspective. In the foreground, the father lovingly embraces his humbled younger son, but behind them we see the older son looking upon the scene with conflicted emotion.

While almost everyone is overjoyed at the son's return, one is not—his older brother. Remember, the younger son had already received his inheritance. For the older one, that meant that everything else belonged to him. Giving anything to the younger son would mean taking it away from the son who had stayed.

He is carrying some emotional baggage.

He was there when his brother demanded his inheritance. He witnessed firsthand the massive weight of grief on his father. Ever since his brother left, he has tried to lift his father's burden. Every day, he has worked to restore his father's broken heart. And now the reckless child is back, and people can't stop lavishing attention on his rebellious brother.

"All these years," he tells his father, "never once have I refused to do a single thing you asked. Yet in all that time, you never celebrated me" (see Luke 15:29).

The loving father responds, "Dear son, all that I have is yours! This is not about comparing rewards or celebrations. This is about healing. This is the moment we have been hoping for all these years. Your brother was dead and is alive again! He was lost but now he is found!" (see Luke 15:31–32).

A PARABLE FOR OUR TIME

My beloved brothers and sisters, dear friends, like all of the Savior's parables, this one is not just about people living long ago. It's about you and me, today. Who among us has not departed from the path of holiness, foolishly thinking we could find more happiness going our own self-centered way? Who among us has not felt humbled, brokenhearted, and desperate for forgiveness and mercy? Perhaps some may even have wondered, "Is it even possible to go back? Will I be labeled forever, rejected, and avoided by my former friends? Is it better to just stay lost? How will God react if I try to return?"

This parable gives us the answer.

Our Heavenly Father will run to us, His heart overflowing with love and compassion. He will embrace us; place a robe around our shoulders, a ring on our finger, and sandals on our feet; and proclaim, "Today we celebrate! For my child, who once was dead, has come back to life!" Heaven will rejoice at our return.

JOY UNSPEAKABLE AND FULL OF GLORY

No matter what may have happened in your life, I echo and proclaim the words of my beloved friend and fellow Apostle President Jeffrey R. Holland: "It is not possible for you to sink lower than the infinite light of Christ's [atoning sacrifice] shines."[3]

Even if choices have taken you far away from the Savior and His Church, the Master Healer stands at the road that leads home, welcoming you. And we as members of the Church of Jesus Christ seek to follow His example and embrace you as our brothers and sisters, as our friends. We rejoice and celebrate with you.

Your return will not diminish the blessings of others. For the

Father's bounty is infinite, and what is given to one does not in the slightest diminish the birthright of others. The Savior taught this doctrine when He offered the parable of the laborers in Matthew 20:1–16. I do not pretend that coming back is an easy thing to do. I can testify of that. It may, in fact, be the toughest choice you will ever make.

But I bear witness that the moment you decide to return and walk in the way of our Savior and Redeemer, His power will enter your life and transform it (see Alma 34:31).

Angels in heaven will rejoice.

And so will we, your family in Christ. After all, we know what it's like to be a prodigal. We all rely daily on the same atoning power of Christ. We know this path, and we will walk with you.

No, our path will not be free from grief, sorrow, or sadness. But we came this far "by the word of Christ with unshaken faith in him, relying wholly upon the merits of him who is mighty to save." And together we will "press forward with a steadfastness in Christ, having a perfect brightness of hope, and a love of God and of all [people]" (2 Nephi 31:19–20). Together we will "rejoice with joy unspeakable and full of glory" (1 Peter 1:8), for Jesus Christ is our strength! (see Psalm 28:7).

It is my prayer that each one of us may hear, in the profound parable of the prodigal son, the Father's voice calling us to enter the road that leads home—that we may have the courage to repent, receive forgiveness, and follow the path that leads back to our compassionate and merciful God.

OUR HEAVENLY FATHER IS A GOD OF NEW BEGINNINGS

As long as we mortals live on this wonderful and beautiful planet, we will make mistakes. Our human actions and failures may even hurt others or wound and damage the earth, our habitat—God's perfect creation.

This is not a surprise to God.

To redeem each of us from our sins and imperfections, our Heavenly Father sent His Only Begotten Son to be born to a mortal woman, live a perfect life, and make a grand, eternal sacrifice that cleanses us from sin and opens the door to holiness, peace, and glory throughout eternity. As we repent, change our ways, and have faith in Him, God will forgive our sins and "remember them no more" (Doctrine and Covenants 58:42). Brothers and sisters, to receive this divine gift of forgiveness, we need to forgive too.

Because of Jesus Christ, our mistakes, our sins, and even our everyday sorrows, pains, disappointments, frustrations, and shortcomings can be healed. Thanks to our Savior, such things need not prevent us from fulfilling our divine destiny!

If you are like me, when you kneel before God at the end of your day and review the choices you have made that day, certain moments may come to mind, and you might think to yourself, "I did all right there." But also, if you are like me, you may recall other moments when perhaps you weren't at your best.

If not for the Atonement of Jesus Christ, such moments would drag us down, discouraging us from moving forward. Instead, the Savior invites us: "Come unto me, all ye that labour and are heavy laden, and I will give you rest" (Matthew 11:28). He offers forgiveness and strength to improve. Because of Jesus Christ, we can leave our burdens behind, resolving each day to better follow Him, the Perfect One.

Our Heavenly Father is the God of new beginnings. Every day, every hour, can be a fresh start—an opportunity to renew ourselves in the Holy Spirit and become better at walking as true and faithful disciples of the Savior. His gospel is the good news that we can begin again; we can become new creatures in Christ (see 2 Corinthians 5:17).

I am not suggesting that we diminish or trivialize our sins and mistakes. We do not brush them under the carpet or try to hide them. On the contrary, to receive God's forgiveness, we must confess our sins. Only when we fully and honestly acknowledge our weaknesses and failures can we learn from them and overcome them. We must humbly assess where we are before we can change course and progress to where we want to be.

In other words, we must repent!

As you partake of the sacrament, you remember the covenant you made at baptism to take the Savior's name upon yourself and to walk in the path of discipleship. You approach the mercy seat of God and, in humility, lay your sins before Him as an offering of sacrifice and plead for His mercy. You recommit to loving and serving Him and to loving and serving others. You ask for His blessing as you dedicate your thoughts and actions to His service.

I testify that you will feel the hand of God stretching out over you. The God of the universe will infuse you with the strength and motivation to do better. There will be mistakes and stumbles in the future. But just as each sunrise signals the beginning of a new day, each time we repent, we make a fresh start on our path of discipleship. We can begin again. Over and over, day after day, we can begin again.

My testimony to you is that God yearns for you to come to Him. His mercy and grace are sufficient to heal your wounds, inspire you to move forward, cleanse you of sin, strengthen you for trials to come, and bless you with hope, wisdom, and His peace.

If you desire it with all your heart, God will guide you through this mortal life, and He will wait with open arms to embrace you in the Resurrection. No matter our shortcomings, no matter our flaws, God can heal, inspire, and cleanse us. For He is the God of new beginnings.

Chapter 4

LIVING IN GRACE AND HOPE

What might living in grace and hope look like for us in our individual paths of discipleship?

When we hear the transcendent truths of the gospel of Jesus Christ, hope and faith begin to blossom inside of us (see Romans 10:17). The more we fill our hearts and minds with the message of the risen Christ, the greater our desire is to follow Him and live His teachings. This, in turn, causes our faith to grow and allows the light of Christ to illuminate our hearts. As it does, we recognize the imperfections in our lives, and we desire to be cleansed of the depressing burdens of sin. We yearn for freedom from guilt, and this inspires us to repent.

Faith and repentance lead to the purifying waters of baptism, where we covenant to take upon us the name of Jesus Christ and walk in His footsteps. To uphold us in the desire to lead a purified and holy life, we are endowed with the baptism of fire—the unspeakable gift of the Holy Ghost, a heavenly Comforter who accompanies and guides us as we walk in the path of righteousness. The more we are filled with the Spirit of God, the more we extend ourselves to others. We become peacemakers in our homes and families, we help our neighbors everywhere, and we reach out in merciful acts of kindness, forgiveness, grace, and long-suffering patience. These are the first steps along the true way of life and fulfillment. This is the peaceable way of the follower of Jesus Christ.

However, being a disciple of Jesus Christ involves much more than talking and preaching of Christ. The Savior Himself restored His Church to help us on the path to become more like Him. The Church of Jesus Christ of Latter-day Saints is structured to provide opportunities to practice the fundamentals of discipleship. Through our participation in the Church, we learn to recognize and act on the promptings of the Holy Spirit. We develop the disposition of reaching out in compassion and kindness to others.

This is an effort of a lifetime, and it requires practice.

Accomplished athletes spend countless hours practicing the fundamentals of their sports. Nurses, networkers, and nuclear engineers become capable and skilled only as they diligently practice their craft.

Now, after this many pages, it seems high time for me to talk about aviation. As an airline captain, I often trained pilots using a flight simulator—a sophisticated machine that replicates the flying experience. The simulator not only helps pilots learn the fundamentals of flying, it also allows them to experience and react to unexpected events they could encounter when they take command of the real aircraft. The same principles of learning apply for disciples of Jesus Christ.

Actively participating in the Church of Jesus Christ and its great variety of opportunities will help us to be better prepared for life's changing circumstances, whatever and however serious they may be. As members of the Church, we are encouraged to immerse ourselves in the words of God through His prophets, ancient and modern. Through sincere and humble prayer to our Heavenly Father, we learn to recognize the voice of the Holy Spirit. We accept calls to serve, teach, plan, minister, and administer. These opportunities allow us to grow in spirit, mind, and character. They will help us prepare to make and keep sacred covenants that will bless us in this life and in the life to come. Certain characteristics will help us immensely as we seek discipleship.

PATIENCE

Patience is one of those characteristics. When I was ten years old and my family became refugees for a second time, and we had to start over again in the western part of Germany, I faced many new challenges. I had always been a good student in school—that is, until we arrived in West Germany. East Germany was occupied by Russia, and West Germany was occupied by Western Allies. The two educational systems were different and aligned with their respective occupational forces. In East Germany, I had been learning Russian as a second language; now, in the West, I had to learn English. This was hard for me. Indeed, there were moments when I truly believed my tongue simply was not made to speak English. Because so much of the curriculum was new and strange to me, I fell behind. For the first time in my life, I began to wonder if I was simply not smart enough for school.

Fortunately, I had a teacher who taught me to be patient. He taught me that steady and consistent work—patient persistence—would help me to learn. Over time, difficult subjects became clearer—even English. Slowly I began to see that if I applied myself consistently, I could learn. It didn't come quickly, but with patience, it did come. From that experience, I learned that patience was far more than simply waiting for something to happen—patience required actively working toward worthwhile goals and not getting discouraged when results didn't appear instantly or without effort.

There is an important concept here: patience is not passive resignation, nor is it failing to act because of our fears. Patience means active waiting and enduring. It means staying with something and doing all that we can—working, hoping, and exercising faith; bearing hardship with fortitude, even when the desires of our hearts are delayed. Patience is not simply enduring; it is enduring well!

Impatience, on the other hand, is a symptom of selfishness. It is a trait of the self-absorbed. It arises from the all-too-prevalent condition called "center of the universe syndrome," which leads people to believe that the world revolves around them and that all others are just supporting cast in the grand theater of mortality in which only they have the starring role.

THE PATH OF PATIENCE

Learning patience means we realize that rarely is there a quick fix or an overnight cure for our struggles.

A friend of mine recently wrote to me, confiding that he was having a difficult time keeping his testimony strong and vibrant. He asked for counsel. I wrote back to him and lovingly suggested a few specific things he could do that would align his life more closely with the teachings of the restored gospel. To my surprise, I heard back from him only a week later. The essence of his letter was this: "I tried what you suggested. It didn't work. What else have you got?"

Brothers and sisters, we have to stay with it. We don't acquire eternal life in a sprint—this is a race of endurance. We have to apply and reapply the divine gospel principles. Day after day we need to make them part of our normal life. Too often we approach the gospel like a farmer who places a seed in the ground in the morning and expects corn on the cob by the afternoon. When Alma compared the word of God to a seed, he explained that the seed grows into a fruit-bearing tree gradually, as a result of our "faith, and [our] diligence, and patience, and long-suffering" (Alma 32:43). There is much to learn of patience in Alma's comparison. It's true that some blessings come right away: soon after we plant the seed in our hearts, it begins to swell and sprout and grow, and by this we know that the seed is good. From the very moment we set foot upon the pathway of discipleship, seen and unseen blessings from God begin to attend us.

But we cannot receive the fulness of those blessings if we "neglect the tree, and take no thought for its nourishment" (Alma 32:38). Knowing that the seed is good is not enough. We must "nourish it with great care, that it may get root" (Alma 32:37). Only then can we partake of the fruit that is "sweet above all that is sweet, and . . . pure above all that is pure" and "feast upon this fruit even until [we] are filled, that [we] hunger not, neither shall [we] thirst" (Alma 32:42).

Discipleship is a journey. We need the refining lessons of the journey to craft our character and purify our hearts. By patiently walking in the path of discipleship, we demonstrate to ourselves the measure of our faith and our willingness to accept God's will rather than ours.

It is not enough merely to speak of Jesus Christ or proclaim that we are His disciples. It is not enough to surround ourselves with symbols of our religion. Discipleship is not a spectator sport. We cannot expect to experience the blessings of faith by standing inactive on the sidelines any more than we can experience the benefits of health by sitting on a sofa watching sporting events on television and giving advice to the athletes. And yet for some, "spectator discipleship" is a preferred if not a primary way of worshipping. Ours is not a second-hand religion. We cannot receive the blessings of the gospel merely by observing the good that others do. We need to get off the sidelines and practice what we preach.

BALANCE: LIKE RIDING A BICYCLE

Another characteristic that helps us is balance. Balance and lift come as we "press forward with a steadfastness in Christ, having a perfect brightness of hope, and a love of God and of all men" (2 Nephi 31:20). My wife, Harriet, and I love to go bicycle riding together. It's a wonderful way to get some exercise while also spending time together. While we're riding, and when I'm not huffing and puffing too much, we enjoy the beautiful world around us and even engage in pleasant conversation. Rarely do we have to pay much attention to keeping our balance on our bicycles. We've been riding long enough that we don't even think about that—it has become normal and natural for us.

But whenever I watch someone learning to ride a bike for the first time, I'm reminded that it's not easy balancing yourself on those two narrow wheels. It takes time. It takes practice. It takes patience. It even takes falling down a time or two. Most of all, those who succeed in balancing on a bicycle learn these important tips:

Don't look at your front wheel.

Look ahead.

Keep your eyes on the road ahead of you. Focus on your destination. And get pedaling. Staying balanced is all about moving forward.

Similar principles apply when it comes to finding balance in our lives as disciples of Jesus Christ. How to distribute your time and energy among your many important tasks will vary from person to person and from one season of life to another. But our common, overall objective is to follow the Way of our Master, Jesus Christ, and return to the presence of our beloved Father in Heaven. This objective must remain constant and consistent, whoever we are and whatever else is happening in our lives. Our children and youth are invited to grow in a balanced way as they follow Jesus Christ, who as a young man "increased in wisdom and stature, and in favour with God and man" (Luke 2:52). We all need to remember that learning takes time. Discipleship is a skill we learn over time.

Now, for those who are avid bicyclists, comparing discipleship to riding a bike may be a helpful analogy. For those who are not, don't worry. I have another analogy I'm sure every man, woman, and child will be able to relate to.

LIFT: LIKE FLYING AN AIRPLANE

Discipleship, like most things in life, can also be compared to flying an airplane. Have you ever stopped to think how amazing it is that a huge passenger jet can actually get off the ground and fly? What is it that keeps these flying machines soaring elegantly through the sky, crossing oceans and continents?

Put simply, an aircraft flies only when air is moving over its wings. That movement creates differences in air pressure that give the plane lift. And how do you get enough air moving over the wings to create lift? The answer is forward thrust. The airplane gains no altitude sitting on the runway. Even on a windy day, enough lift isn't created unless the airplane is moving forward, with enough thrust to counteract the forces holding it back. Just as forward momentum keeps a bicycle balanced and upright, moving forward helps an aircraft overcome the pull of gravity and drag with sufficient lift.

What does this mean for us as disciples of Jesus Christ? It means that if we want to find balance in life, and if we want the Savior to lift us heavenward, then our commitment to Him and His gospel can't be casual or occasional. Like the widow at Jerusalem, we must offer Him our whole souls. Our offering may be small, but it must come from our heart and soul.

Being a disciple of Jesus Christ is not just one of many things we do. The Savior is the motivating power behind *all* that we do. He is not a rest stop in our journey. He is not a scenic byway or even a major landmark. He is "the way, the truth, and the life: no man cometh unto the Father, but by [Jesus Christ]" (John 14:6). That is the Way and our ultimate destination. Balance and lift come as we "press forward with a steadfastness in Christ, having a perfect brightness of hope, and a love of God and of all" (2 Nephi 31:20).

SACRIFICE AND CONSECRATION

And what about the many tasks and responsibilities that make our lives so busy? Spending time with loved ones, going to school or preparing for an occupation, earning a living, caring for family, serving in the community—where does it all fit in? The Savior reassures us:

"Your heavenly Father knoweth that ye have need of all these things. But seek ye first the kingdom of God and his righteousness, and all these things shall be added unto you" (3 Nephi 13:32–33; see also Matthew 6:32–33).

Joseph Smith's Translation of Matthew 6:38 provides additional insight: "Seek not the things of this world but seek ye first to build up the kingdom of God, and to establish his righteousness."[1]

But that doesn't mean it's easy. It requires both *sacrifice* and *consecration*. It requires letting some things *go* and letting other things *grow*. One example comes from our prophet, President Russell M. Nelson. When he was at the height of his professional career as a heart surgeon, he was called as stake president. Elders Spencer W. Kimball and LeGrand Richards extended the call. Recognizing the demands of his professional life, they said to him, "If you feel that you are too busy and shouldn't accept the call, then that's your privilege." He answered that his decision about whether or not to serve when called was made long ago, when he and his wife made temple covenants with the Lord. "We made a commitment then," he said, "to 'seek . . . first the kingdom of God, and his righteousness' [Matthew 6:33], feeling confident that everything else would be added unto us, as the Lord promised."[2] When we put God first, everything else falls into place.

Sacrifice and *consecration* are two heavenly laws that we covenant to obey in the holy temple. These two laws are similar but not identical. To *sacrifice* means to give something up in favor of something more valuable. Anciently, God's people sacrificed the firstlings of their flocks in honor of the coming Messiah. Throughout history, faithful Saints have sacrificed personal desires, comforts, and even their lives for the Savior.

THE WIDOW'S MITE

Perhaps we question whether we have anything of value to give. But think, just days before He gave His life for us, Jesus Christ was at the temple in Jerusalem, watching people make donations to the temple treasury. "Many that were rich cast in much," but then, along came a poor widow, "and she threw in two mites." It was such a small amount, it would hardly be worth recording.

And yet this seemingly inconsequential donation caught the Savior's attention. In fact, it impressed Him so deeply that "he called unto him his disciples, and saith unto them, Verily I say unto you, That this poor widow hath cast more in, than all they which have cast into the treasury: For all they did cast in of their abundance; but she of her want did cast in all that she had, even all her living" (Mark 12:41–44).

With this simple observation, the Savior taught us how offerings are measured in His kingdom—and it's quite different from the way we usually measure things. To the Lord, the value of the donation was measured not by the effect it had on the treasury but by the effect it had on the heart of the donor.

In praising this faithful widow, the Savior gave us a standard to measure our discipleship in all of its many expressions. Jesus taught that our offering may be large or it may be small, but either way, it must be our *heartfelt all*.

This principle is echoed in the plea of the Book of Mormon prophet Amaleki: "Come unto Christ, who is the Holy One of Israel, and partake of his salvation, and the power of his redemption. Yea, come unto him, and offer your whole souls as an offering unto him" (Omni 1:26).

But how is this possible? To many of us, such a standard of whole-souled commitment seems out of reach. We are already stretched so thin. What does this mean for us as disciples of Jesus Christ? It means that if we want to find balance in life, and if we want the Savior to lift us heavenward, then our commitment to Him and His gospel can't be casual or occasional. Like the widow at Jerusalem, we must offer Him our whole souls. Our offering may be small, but it must come from our heart and soul.

We all have things, large and small, we need to sacrifice in order to follow Jesus Christ more completely. President Nelson spoke of "the need for each of us to remove, with the Savior's help, the old debris in our lives. . . . I invite you to pray," he said, "to identify the debris you should remove from your life so you can become more worthy."[3] Our sacrifices show what we truly value. The scriptures say that, to God, our sacrifices are more sacred than our accomplishments (see Doctrine and Covenants 117:13). This may be one reason the Lord valued the widow's mites more than the contribution of the wealthy. The former was a sacrifice, which had a purifying effect on the giver. The latter, while it may have accomplished more monetarily, may not have been a sacrifice, and could leave the giver unchanged. Sacrifices are sacred and honored by the Lord.

Consecration is different from sacrifice in at least one important way. When we consecrate something, we don't leave it to be consumed upon the altar. Rather, we put it to use in the Lord's service. We dedicate it to Him and His holy purposes. We receive the talents that the Lord has given us and strive to increase them, manifold, to become even more helpful in building the Lord's kingdom (see Matthew 25:14–30).

Very few of us will ever be asked to *sacrifice* our lives for the Savior. But we are all invited to *consecrate* our lives to Him.

ONE WORK, ONE JOY, ONE PURPOSE

As we seek to purify our lives and look unto Christ in every thought (see Doctrine and Covenants 6:36), everything else begins to align. Life no longer feels like a long list of separate efforts held in tenuous balance.

Over time, it all becomes one work.

One joy.

One holy purpose.

It is the work of loving and serving God. It is loving and serving God's children. In this way, we see in our lives a fulfillment of the prophecy of the Apostle Paul: "In the dispensation of the fulness of times [God will] gather together in one all things in Christ, both which are in heaven, and which are on earth; even in him" (Ephesians 1:10).

When we look at our lives and see a hundred things to do, we feel overwhelmed. When we see one thing—loving and serving God and His children, in a hundred different ways—then we can work on those things with joy.

This is how we offer our whole souls—by sacrificing anything that's holding us back and consecrating the rest to the Lord and His purposes.

RELYING ON THE ATONEMENT OF JESUS CHRIST

Jesus Christ has made a perfect Atonement for mankind. It is the message of love, hope, and mercy that there is a reconciliation of man with God.

Christ came to save us. If we have taken a wrong course, the Atonement of Jesus Christ can give us the assurance that sin is not a point of no return. A safe return is possible if we will follow God's plan for our salvation.

We have received this plan from the highest authority in the universe, even God, our Heavenly Father. This plan was prepared from before the foundation of the earth. It is a great plan of happiness, a plan of mercy, a plan of redemption, a plan of salvation. This plan enables us to experience a physical existence, including mortality, a time of probation, and to return to the presence of God and live in eternal happiness and glory. It is explained in the doctrine of the restored gospel of Jesus Christ.

Following this plan has beautiful eternal consequences for us individually, for our families, for generations to come, and even for generations who went before. The plan includes divine reconciliation and forgiveness.

True repentance blesses our lives with the effects of the Savior's Atonement: we feel God's forgiveness and His peace, and our guilt and sorrow are lifted away; we enjoy the influence of the Spirit in greater abundance; and we are better prepared to live with our Heavenly Father.

President Spencer W. Kimball taught: "The essence of the miracle of forgiveness is that it brings peace to the previously anxious, restless, frustrated, perhaps tormented soul. . . . God will wipe away . . . the tears of anguish, and remorse, . . . and fear, and guilt."[4]

Jesus promised, "Peace I leave with you, my peace I give unto you: . . . Let not your heart be troubled, neither let it be afraid" (John 14:27).

The prophet Alma, who was reclaimed from sin to happiness by God's forgiveness, declared, "Wickedness never was happiness" (Alma 41:10). He had witnessed the bitter pains of sin, but he also spoke with excitement about the happiness that accompanies true repentance and forgiveness: "Yea, I say unto you, . . . there can be nothing so exquisite and sweet as was my joy" (Alma 36:21). Alma concluded with powerful and wise counsel to all who seek forgiveness: "And now, . . . I desire that ye should let these things trouble you no more, and only let your sins trouble you, with that trouble which shall bring you down unto repentance" (Alma 42:29).

Once we have truly repented, Christ will take away the burden of guilt for our sins. We can know for ourselves that we have been forgiven and made clean. The Holy Ghost will verify this to us; He is the Sanctifier. No other testimony of forgiveness can be greater.

The Lord said, "He that repents and *does the commandments* of the Lord shall be forgiven" (Doctrine and Covenants 1:32; emphasis added). And He said, "Be faithful and diligent . . . and I will encircle thee in the arms of my love" (Doctrine and Covenants 6:20). He also declared, "Behold, he who has repented of his sins, the same is forgiven, and I, the Lord, remember them no more" (Doctrine and Covenants 58:42).

Satan will try to make us believe that our sins are not forgiven because *we* can remember them. Satan is a liar; he tries to blur our vision and lead us away from the path of repentance and forgiveness. God did not promise that *we* would not remember our sins. Remembering will help us avoid making the same mistakes again. But if we stay true and faithful and continue living in the hope of our Savior and receiving His grace, the memory of our sins will be softened over time. This will be part of the needed healing and sanctification process. Alma testified that after he cried out to Jesus for mercy, he could still remember his sins, but the memory of his sins no longer distressed and tortured him, because he knew he had been forgiven (see Alma 36:17–19).

I acknowledge that your path will at times be difficult. But I give you this promise in the name of the Lord: rise up and follow in the footsteps of our Redeemer and Savior, and one day you will look back and be filled with eternal gratitude that you chose to trust Him and His power to lift you up and give you strength.

Chapter 5

LOVING GOD AND OUR NEIGHBORS

When a Pharisee asked Jesus which was the greatest of the commandments, the Savior established once and for all what our priorities as individuals and as a Church should be:

1. Love God (see Matthew 22:37).

2. Love your neighbor (see Matthew 22:39; see also verses 34–40).

That is the center of the gospel. It should be the center of our every effort as a Church and as disciples of Jesus Christ. And it is essential to continually receiving the Lord's grace in our lives.

When we wonder where we should put our focus as parents, siblings, Church leaders, ministering brothers and sisters, and members of The Church of Jesus Christ of Latter-day Saints, it is already decided:

1. Love God.

2. Love your neighbor.

I suppose that when we descended from the realms of heavenly glory to this earth, we did so with a sense of anticipation and perhaps a little apprehension. After all, we would not remember our premortal life. We would be shut out from God's presence (see Moses 5:4). How would we find our way back to our beloved Heavenly Father? That was our overarching desire—to seek God, find Him, love Him, and follow Him.

We knew that there would be many unexpected challenges. Perhaps we even anticipated that the odds might be stacked against us. But we trusted our Father, and we were eager to prove our loyalty to Him (see Abraham 3:25).

Even so, it is easy to get caught up in other things. Even good things can distract us from our primary purpose. And I am not referring only to worldly distractions. Let's face it: the canvas of the gospel is so broad and rich that we could spend a lifetime studying it and scarcely scratch the surface. We all have topics or principles that interest us more than others. Naturally, those are the things we gravitate toward, speak about, and emphasize in our lives.

Are those principles important? Certainly. But we would do well to consider whether they are the *most* important.

The ancient Pharisees compiled hundreds of rules and commandments from sacred writings. They made a great effort to catalog them, comply with them, and enforce them with precision. They believed that exact obedience to the smallest of these procedures would lead people to God.

Where did they go wrong?

They lost sight of the center. They lost sight of what was of most worth for their eternal purpose. They saw the multitude of rules as ends in themselves instead of as the means to an end.

Are we susceptible to the same mistake today? If we were to brainstorm, I am sure we could compile a list of latter-day expectations that would rival those amassed anciently. It is not to say that these rules and gospel topics are not important or valuable. No. They have a purpose. They are part of the whole. They can lead us *to* the center, but they are not *the* center. They are branches of the tree, but they are not the tree. And if they ever become separated from the tree, they will have no life. They will not bring forth fruit that will remain. They will wither and die.

In one of His final discourses in mortality, Jesus taught His disciples what would happen at the Final Judgment, explaining that our eternal future will depend largely upon how we have treated others (see Matthew 25:31–40). When we meet the Savior at the judgment bar, we will account for how we lived the two great commandments.

- Did we truly seek God?
- Did we love Him with all our heart, might, mind, and strength? (see Doctrine and Covenants 59:5).
- Did we love our families, friends, and neighbors? How did we manifest that love?

We could actually make this a two-point diagnostic exam to evaluate ourselves as disciples of Jesus Christ and servants in His kingdom:

How can we be better disciples?

1. Love God.

2. Love our neighbor.

How can we be happier?

1. Love God.

2. Love our neighbor.

How can we better magnify our callings in the Church?

1. Love God.

2. Love our neighbor.

Yes, we cherish all the principles of the gospel. We "live by every word that proceedeth forth from the mouth of God" (Doctrine and Covenants 84:44). And yet we must always remember that "all the law and the prophets" point to the two great commandments (Matthew 22:40).

As Relief Society General President Sister Camille N. Johnson wisely taught, "When we prioritize the first and second great commandments—we are letting God prevail. When we prioritize love of God and love of our neighbor and family—then the things that don't have eternal significance drop off the list."[1] This is the bull's-eye of the gospel of Jesus Christ. It is the foundation of who we are as His followers.

IF JESUS WERE HERE

Suppose Jesus came to your ward, to your branch, or to your home today. What would that be like?

He would see right into your heart. Outward appearances would lose their importance. He would know you as you are. He would know your heart's desires.

The meek and the humble He would lift.

The sick He would heal.

The doubting He would infuse with faith and courage to believe.

He would teach us to open our hearts to God and reach out to others.

He would recognize and honor honesty, humility, integrity, faithfulness, compassion, and charity.

One look into His eyes and we would never be the same. We would be forever changed. Transformed by the profound realization that, indeed, God is among us.

I look back with kindness on the young man I was during my growing-up years. If I could go back in time, I would comfort him and tell him to stay on the right track and keep searching. And I would ask him to invite Jesus Christ into his life, for God is among us!

To all who are searching for answers, truth, and happiness, I offer the same counsel: keep searching with faith and patience (see Alma 41:4–5, 10–11).

Ask, and you will receive. Knock, and it will be opened unto you (see Doctrine and Covenants 88:63). Trust the Lord (see Proverbs 3:5).

In our daily life it is our paramount task and blessed opportunity to encounter God.

As we set aside pride and approach His throne with a broken heart and a contrite spirit, He will draw near to us.

As we seek to follow Jesus Christ and walk the path of discipleship, line upon line, the day will come that we will experience that unimaginable gift of receiving a fulness of joy. Yet, He does not leave us destitute in the here and now; He offers us hope and grace through His Son. And living in that hope and grace is "all we can do" (2 Nephi 25:23). Living in hope and grace will bring us enduring joy. My beloved friends, your Heavenly Father loves you with a perfect love. He has proven His love in endless ways, but above all by giving His Only Begotten Son as a sacrifice and as a gift to His children to make the return to our heavenly parents a reality.

REACH OUT IN LOVE TO OTHERS

There is something interesting, almost paradoxical, about this path we have each chosen: the only way for us to progress in our gospel adventure is to help others progress as well.

To help others *is* the path of discipleship. Faith, hope, love, compassion, and service define and refine us as disciples.

Through your efforts to help the poor and the needy, to reach out to those in distress, your own character is purified and forged, your spirit is enlarged, and you walk a little taller.

But this love cannot come with expectations of repayment. It cannot be the kind of service that expects recognition, adulation, or favor.

True disciples of Jesus Christ love God and His children without expectation of something in return. We love those who disappoint us, who don't like us. Even those who ridicule, abuse, and seek to hurt us.

When you fill your hearts with the pure love of Christ, you leave no room for rancor, judgment, and shaming. You keep God's commandments because you love Him. In the process, you slowly become more Christlike in your thoughts and deeds. And what adventure could be greater than this?

LORD, IS IT I?

It was our beloved Savior's final night in mortality, the evening before He would offer Himself a ransom for all humankind. As He broke bread with His disciples, He said something that must have filled their hearts with great alarm and deep sadness. "One of you shall betray me," He told them.

The disciples didn't question the truth of what He said. Nor did they look around, point to someone else, and ask, "Is it him?"

Instead, "they were exceeding sorrowful, and began every one of them to say unto him, *Lord, is it I?*" (Matthew 26:21–22; emphasis added).

I wonder what each of us would do if we were in the room when the Savior made that statement. Would we look at those around us and say in our hearts, "He's probably talking about Brother so-and-so. I've always wondered about him," or "I'm glad Sister so-and-so is here. She really needs to hear this message"? Or would we, like those disciples of old, look inward and ask that penetrating question: "Is it I?" In these simple words, *"Lord, is it I?"* lies the beginning of wisdom and the pathway to personal conversion and lasting change.

A PARABLE OF DANDELIONS

Once there was a man who enjoyed taking evening walks around his neighborhood. He particularly looked forward to walking past his neighbor's house. This neighbor kept his lawn perfectly manicured, flowers always in bloom, the trees healthy and shady. It was obvious that the neighbor made every effort to have a beautiful lawn.

But one day as the man was walking past his neighbor's house, he noticed in the middle of this beautiful lawn a single, enormous, yellow dandelion weed.

It looked so out of place that it surprised him. Why didn't his neighbor pull it out? Couldn't he see it? Didn't he know that the dandelion could cast seeds that could give root to dozens of additional weeds?

This solitary dandelion bothered him beyond description, and he wanted to do something about it. Should he just pluck it out? Or spray it with weed killer? Perhaps if he went under cover of night, he could remove it secretly.

These thoughts totally occupied his mind as he walked toward his own home. He entered his house without even glancing at his own front yard—which was blanketed with hundreds of yellow dandelions.

BEAMS AND MOTES

Does this story remind us of the words of the Savior?

"Why beholdest thou the mote that is in thy brother's eye, but considerest not the beam that is in thine own eye? . . .

" . . . First cast out the beam out of thine own eye; and then shalt thou see clearly to cast out the mote out of thy brother's eye" (Matthew 7:3, 5).

This business of beams and motes seems to be closely related to our inability to see ourselves clearly. I'm not sure why we are able to diagnose and recommend remedies for other people's ills so well, while we often have difficulty seeing our own.

Some years ago there was a news story about a man who believed that if he rubbed lemon juice on his face, it would make him invisible to cameras. So he put lemon juice all over his face, went out, and robbed two banks. Not much later he was arrested when his image was broadcast over the evening news. When police showed the man the videos of himself from the security cameras, he couldn't believe his eyes. "But I had lemon juice on my face!" he protested.[2]

When a scientist at Cornell University heard about this story, he was intrigued that a man could be so painfully unaware of his own incompetence. To determine whether this was a general problem, two researchers invited college students to participate in a series of tests on various life skills and then asked them to rate how they did. The students who performed poorly were the least accurate at evaluating their own performance—some of them estimating their scores to be five times higher than they actually were.[3]

This study has been replicated in numerous ways, confirming over and over again the same conclusion: many of us have a difficult time seeing ourselves as we truly are, and even successful people overestimate their own contribution and underestimate the contributions that others make.[4]

It might not be so significant to overestimate how well we drive a car or how far we can drive a golf ball. But when we start believing that our contributions at home, at work, and at church are greater than they actually are, we blind ourselves to blessings and opportunities to improve ourselves in significant and profound ways.

SPIRITUAL BLIND SPOTS

An acquaintance of mine used to live in a ward with some of the highest activity statistics in the Church—attendance was high, ministering visit numbers were high, Primary children were always well behaved, ward dinners included fantastic food that members rarely spilled on the meetinghouse floor, and I think there were never any arguments at Church sports.

My friend and his wife were subsequently called on a mission. When they returned three years later, this couple was astonished to learn that during the time they were away serving, eleven marriages within the ward had ended in divorce.

While there are situations in which divorce is an appropriate and necessary option, in many marriages, a spiritual reorientation and a renewed focus on the Savior and on eternal covenants could help avoid this painful outcome. In the case of this particular ward, there was every outward indication of faithfulness and strength, but something unfortunate was happening in the hearts and lives of some members. And the troubling thing is that this situation is not unique. Such terrible and often unnecessary things happen when members of the Church become disengaged from gospel principles. They may appear on the outside to be disciples of Jesus Christ, but on the inside their hearts have separated from their Savior and His teachings. They have gradually turned away from the things of the Spirit and moved toward the things of the world.

Once-worthy priesthood holders start to tell themselves that the Church is a good thing for those who need it but that they themselves are fine without it. Some convince themselves that their busy schedules or unique circumstances make them exempt from the daily acts of devotion and service that would keep them close to the Spirit. In this age of self-justification and narcissism, it is easy to become quite creative at coming up with excuses for not regularly approaching God in prayer, procrastinating the study of the scriptures, avoiding Church meetings and home evenings, or not paying an honest tithe.

My friends, will you please look inside your hearts and ask the simple question: *"Lord, is it I?"*

Have you disengaged—even slightly—from "the . . . gospel of the blessed God, which was committed to [your] trust"? (1 Timothy 1:11). Have you allowed "the god of this world" to darken your minds to "the light of the glorious gospel of Christ"? (2 Corinthians 4:4).

My beloved friends, ask yourselves, "Where is my treasure?"

Is your heart set on the convenient things of this world, or is it focused on the teachings of the diligent Jesus Christ? "For where your treasure is, there will your heart be also" (Luke 12:34).

Does the Spirit of God dwell in your hearts? Are you "rooted and grounded" in the love of God and of your neighbor? Do you devote sufficient time and creativity to bringing happiness to your marriage, family, and friendships? Do you give your energies to the sublime goal of comprehending and living "the breadth, and length, and depth, and height" of the restored gospel of Jesus Christ? (Ephesians 3:17–18).

If it is your great desire to cultivate Christlike attributes of "faith, virtue, knowledge, temperance, patience, brotherly kindness, godliness, charity, humility, [and service]," Heavenly Father will make you an instrument in His hands unto the salvation of many souls (Doctrine and Covenants 4:6).

CONFLICT IS INEVITABLE; CONTENTION IS A CHOICE

Have you noticed that in many movies there comes a moment when someone says, "At least things can't get any worse"? As soon as you hear those words, you know that things are about to fall apart. Do you ever feel like a character in one of those movies?

Just when it seems as though you have faced all the trials and heartaches you can handle, bigger ones come along. These conflicts come in a variety of shapes and sizes: An unwanted medical diagnosis. A wandering child or friend. The loss of a job. The passing of a loved one. A global pandemic.

Sometimes we think how pleasant life would be if only we didn't have so much opposition.

Our Lord Jesus Christ—our model of perfection—did not live a life free of conflict. He was opposed throughout His ministry, and in His final hours He was betrayed by a friend, accused by false witnesses, slandered, beaten, bloodied, and crucified. What was His response? To some, He did not speak a word. To others, He spoke the simple truth—not in anger but with calm majesty. As others contended with Him, He stood in His place—trusting in His Father, calm in His testimony, and firm in the truth.

Conflict is inevitable. It is a condition of mortality. It is part of our test. Contention, however, is a choice. It is one way that some people choose to respond to conflict. When we contend with others, we cause discord, dissension, resentment, and even rage. Harmful emotions almost always accompany contention: anger, hurt, jealousy, hostility, revenge, and malice—to name just a few.

Our world overflows with contention. We have 24/7 access to

LOVING GOD AND OUR NEIGHBORS

it: on the news, on social media, and even, at times, in our relation-ships with those we love. We cannot adjust the volume on others' bitterness, wrath, or rage. We can, however, choose our response. Of course this is easy to say and difficult to do. To refrain from con-tending with those who contend requires great discipline. But that's what it means to be a disciple. Jesus taught: "He that hath the spirit of contention is not of me, but is of the devil, who is the father of contention. . . . This is my doctrine, that such things should be done away" (3 Nephi 11:29–30).

When God speaks—even when He calls us to repentance—His voice is not likely to be "a voice of thunder, neither . . . a voice of a great tumultuous noise, but . . . a still voice of perfect mildness, . . . [like] a whisper . . . [that pierces] even to the very soul" (Helaman 5:30). As followers of Jesus Christ, we follow this example. We do not shame or attack others. We seek to love God and serve our neighbors. We strive to extend to others the same grace that the Savior so mercifully bestows upon us. We seek to joyfully keep God's commandments and live by gospel principles. And we invite others to do the same.

We cannot force anyone to change. But we can love them. We can be an example of what the restored gospel of Jesus Christ is all about. And we can invite all to come and belong. When others throw insults at us, do we return fire? There is a better way—the Lord's way! To some, we say nothing. To others, we state with quiet dignity who we are, what we believe, and why we believe. We stand confident in our faith in God, trusting that He will uphold us in our trials. Let us emulate the gentle Christ by learning to love God and reaching out to bless others. Yes, there will still be conflict. But our all-powerful Father in Heaven has promised that He will fight our battles for us.[5]

WHEN RELATIONSHIPS GO BAD

Strained and broken relationships are as old as humankind itself. Ancient Cain was the first who allowed the cancer of bitterness and malice to canker his heart. He tilled the ground of his soul with envy and hatred and allowed these feelings to ripen until he did the unthinkable—murdering his own brother and becoming, in the process, the father of Satan's lies (see Moses 5:16–32).

Since those first days, the spirit of envy and hatred has led to some of the most tragic stories in history. It turned Saul against David, the sons of Jacob against their brother Joseph, Laman and Lemuel against Nephi, and Amalickiah against Moroni.

I imagine that every person on earth has been affected in some way by the destructive spirit of contention, resentment, and revenge. Perhaps there are even times when we recognize this spirit in ourselves. When we feel hurt, angry, or envious, it is quite easy to judge other people, often assigning dark motives to their actions in order to justify our own feelings of resentment.

Of course, we know this is wrong. The doctrine is clear. We all depend on the Savior; none of us can be saved without Him. Christ's Atonement is infinite and eternal. Forgiveness for *our* sins comes with conditions. We must repent, and we must be willing to forgive others. Jesus taught: "Forgive one another; for he that forgiveth not . . . [stands] condemned before the Lord; for there remaineth in him the greater sin" (Doctrine and Covenants 64:9) and "Blessed are the merciful: for they shall obtain mercy" (Matthew 5:7).

Of course, these words seem perfectly reasonable—when applied to someone else. We can so clearly and easily see the harmful results that come when *others* judge and hold grudges. And we certainly don't like it when people judge us.

But when it comes to our own prejudices and grievances, we too often justify our anger as righteous and our judgment as reliable and only appropriate. Though we cannot look into another's heart, we assume that we know a bad motive or even a bad person when we see one. We make exceptions when it comes to our own bitterness because we feel that, in our case, we have all the information we need to hold someone else in contempt.

The Apostle Paul, in his letter to the Romans, said that those who pass judgment on others are "inexcusable." The moment we judge someone else, he explained, we condemn ourselves, for none is without sin (Romans 2:1). Refusing to forgive is a grievous sin— one the Savior warned against. Jesus's own disciples had "sought occasion against one another and forgave not one another in their hearts; and for this evil they were afflicted and sorely chastened" (Doctrine and Covenants 64:8).

Our Savior has spoken so clearly on this subject that there is little room for private interpretation. "I, the Lord, will forgive whom I will forgive," but then He said, " . . . of you it is *required* to forgive *all*" (Doctrine and Covenants 64:10; emphasis added).

May I add a footnote here? When the Lord requires that we forgive all, that includes forgiving ourselves. Sometimes, of all the people in the world, the one who is the hardest to forgive—as well as perhaps the one who is most in need of our forgiveness—is the person looking back at us in the mirror.

THE BOTTOM LINE

This topic of judging others could actually be taught in a two-word sermon. When it comes to hating, gossiping, ignoring, ridiculing, holding grudges, or wanting to cause harm, please apply the following:

Stop it!

It's that simple. We simply have to stop judging others and re-place judgmental thoughts and feelings with a heart full of love for God and His children. God is our Father. We are His children. We are all brothers and sisters. I don't know exactly how to articulate this point of *not judging others* with sufficient eloquence, passion, and persuasion to make it stick. I can quote scripture, I can try to expound doctrine, and I will even quote a bumper sticker I recently saw. It was attached to the back of a car whose driver appeared to be a little rough around the edges, but the words on the sticker taught an insightful lesson. It read, "Don't judge me because I sin differently than you."

Sister Reyna I. Aburto, former counselor in the Relief Society General Presidency, similarly instructed us when she taught, "Let us follow the Savior's path and increase our compassion, diminish our tendency to judge, and stop being the inspectors of the spirituality of others."[6]

We must recognize that we are all imperfect—that we are beggars before God. Haven't we all, at one time or another, meekly approached the mercy seat and pleaded for grace? Haven't we wished with all the energy of our souls for mercy—to be forgiven for the mistakes we have made and the sins we have committed?

Because we all depend on the mercy of God, how can we deny to others any measure of the grace we so desperately desire for ourselves? My beloved brothers and sisters, should we not forgive as we wish to be forgiven?

Is this difficult to do?

Yes, of course.

Forgiving ourselves and others is not easy. In fact, for most of us it requires a major change in our attitude and way of thinking—even a change of heart. But there is good news. This "mighty change" of heart is exactly what the gospel of Jesus Christ is designed to bring into our lives (Mosiah 5:2).

How is it done? Through the love of God.

When our hearts are filled with the love of God, something good and pure happens to us. We "keep his commandments: and his commandments are not grievous. For whatsoever is born of God overcometh the world" (1 John 5:3–4).

The more we allow the love of God to govern our minds and emotions—the more we allow our love for our Heavenly Father to swell within our hearts—the easier it is to love others with the pure love of Christ. As we open our hearts to the glowing dawn of the love of God, the darkness and cold of animosity and envy will eventually fade.

As always, Christ is our exemplar. In His teachings as in His life, He showed us the way. He forgave the wicked, the vulgar, and those who sought to hurt and to do Him harm.

Jesus said it is easy to love those who love us; even the wicked can do *that*. But Jesus Christ taught a higher law. His words echo through the centuries and are meant for us today. They are meant for all who desire to be His disciples. They are meant for you and me: "Love your enemies, bless them that curse you, do good to them that hate you, and pray for them which despitefully use you, and persecute you" (Matthew 5:44; see also verses 45–47).

When our hearts are filled with the love of God, we become "kind one to another, tenderhearted, forgiving [each other], even as God for Christ's sake [forgave us]" (Ephesians 4:32).

The pure love of Christ can remove the scales of resentment and wrath from our eyes, allowing us to see others the way our Heavenly Father sees us: as flawed and imperfect mortals who have potential and worth far beyond our capacity to imagine. Because God loves us so much, we too must love and forgive each other.

THE WAY OF THE DISCIPLE

My dear brothers and sisters, consider the following questions as a self-test:

Do you harbor a grudge against someone else?

Do you gossip, even when what you say may be true?

Do you exclude, push away, or punish others because of something they have done?

Do you secretly envy another?

Do you wish to cause harm to someone?

If you answered yes to any of these questions, you may want to apply the two-word sermon from earlier: stop it!

In a world of accusations and unfriendliness, it is easy to gather and cast stones. But before we do so, let us remember the words of the One who is our Master and model: "He that is without sin among you, let him first cast a stone" (John 8:7).

Brothers and sisters, let us put down our stones.

Let us be kind.

Let us forgive.

Let us talk peacefully with each other.

Let the love of God fill our hearts.

"Let us do good unto all" (Galatians 6:10).

The Savior promised: "Give, and it shall be given unto you; good measure, pressed down, and shaken together, and running over. . . . For with the same measure that [you use] it shall be measured to you again" (Luke 6:38). Shouldn't this promise be enough to always focus our efforts on acts of kindness, forgiveness, and charity instead of on any negative behavior?

Let us, as disciples of Jesus Christ, return good for evil (see Matthew 5:39–41). Let us not seek revenge or allow our wrath to overcome us.

"For it is written, Vengeance is mine; I will repay, saith the Lord. Therefore if thine enemy hunger, feed him; if he thirst, give him drink. . . . Be not overcome of evil, but overcome evil with good" (Romans 12:19–21).

Remember: in the end, it is the merciful who obtain mercy (see Matthew 5:7).

As members of The Church of Jesus Christ of Latter-day Saints, wherever we may be, let us be known as a people who "have love one to another" (John 13:35).

THE EXAMINED LIFE

None of us likes to admit when we are drifting off the right course. Often we try to avoid looking deeply into our souls and confronting our weaknesses, limitations, and fears. Consequently, when we do examine our lives, we look through the filter of biases, excuses, and stories we tell ourselves in order to justify unworthy thoughts and actions.

But being able to see ourselves clearly is essential to our spiritual growth and well-being. If our weaknesses and shortcomings remain obscured in the shadows, then the redeeming power of the Savior cannot heal them and make them strengths (see Ether 12:27). Ironically, our blindness toward our human weaknesses will also make us blind to the divine potential that our Father yearns to nurture within each of us.

So how can we shine the pure light of God's truth into our souls and see ourselves as He sees us?

May I suggest that the holy scriptures and the talks given at general conference are an effective mirror we can hold up for self-examination.

As you hear or read the words of the ancient and modern prophets, refrain from thinking about how the words apply to someone else and ask the simple question: *"Lord, is it I?"*

We must approach our Eternal Father with broken hearts and

teachable minds. We must be willing to learn and to change. And, oh, how much we gain by committing to live the life our Heavenly Father intends for us.

Those who do *not* wish to learn and change probably *will not* and most likely will begin to wonder whether the Church has anything to offer them.

But those who want to improve and progress, those who learn of the Savior and desire to be like Him, those who humble themselves as a little child and seek to bring their thoughts and actions into harmony with our Father in Heaven—they will experience the miracle of the Savior's Atonement. They will surely feel God's resplendent Spirit. They will taste the indescribable joy that is the fruit of a meek and humble heart. They will be blessed with the desire and discipline to become true disciples of Jesus Christ.

THE POWER OF GOOD

Over the course of my life, I have had the opportunity to rub shoulders with some of the most competent and intelligent men and women this world has to offer. When I was younger, I was impressed by those who were educated, accomplished, successful, and applauded by the world. But over the years, I have come to the realization that I am far more impressed by those wonderful and blessed souls who are truly good and without guile.

And isn't that what the gospel is all about and does for us? It is the good news, and it helps us to become good.

The words of the Apostle James apply to us today:

"God resisteth the proud, but giveth grace unto the humble. . . .

"Humble yourselves in the sight of the Lord, and he shall lift you up" (James 4:6, 10).

We must put aside our pride, see beyond our vanity, and in humility ask, *"Lord, is it I?"*

And if the Lord's answer happens to be, "Yes, there are things you must improve, things I can help you to overcome," I pray that we will accept this answer, humbly acknowledge our sins and shortcomings, and then change our ways by becoming better husbands and wives, better mothers and fathers, better daughters and sons. May we from this time forward seek with all our might to walk steadfastly in the Savior's blessed way—for seeing ourselves clearly is the beginning of wisdom.

As we do so, our bountiful God will lead us by the hand; we will "be made strong, and blessed from on high" (Doctrine and Covenants 1:28).

My beloved friends, a first step on this wondrous and fulfilling path of true discipleship starts with our asking the simple question:

"Lord, is it I?"

Chapter 6

OVERCOMING DISCOURAGEMENT

In my youth, my level of confidence seemed to fluctuate almost daily. Some days I thought I could take on the whole world, and the next day I felt down and discouraged. Moroni offers us another explanation for the source of many of our challenges and the reason we sometimes do not feel hopeful:

"And if ye have no hope ye must needs be in despair; and despair [discouragement, frustration] cometh because of iniquity" (Moroni 10:22).

That may be a very tough statement to read. We might initially react by saying, "Well, I'm not sinning. I'm keeping the commandments. So why am I discouraged?"

I believe the Lord is telling us in this verse that as flawed humans in a mortal world, we have not gained total control of our body, spirit, appetites, passions, or even our minds and the way we think about things. We have not perfected ourselves in having control over the miraculous mechanism of our body and mind. But as we strive each day to overcome the natural man or woman and become a little more Christlike, we also find ourselves overcoming despair and filling our lives with hope.

In all of our efforts, a steadfast focus on the Lord will instill in us the faith and the courage to go forward and do the right thing. Wherever you are in your life, you are free to make choices. Many of the small daily choices we make have long-lasting consequences that are deeply connected to gospel principles. For instance, "Do I need to get up every single Sunday and attend my Church meetings, or can I miss them once in a while?" "Do I have to study the scriptures every day during a time when I am so busy?" "Can I sometimes skip over my prayers to get a little more sleep?"

These seemingly small and simple decisions carry great consequences over time. They also carry the potential of bringing great hope or discouragement into your life. May I suggest a few principles that will help you to overcome or avoid discouragement.

PRAY

There might be a certain percentage reading this book who did not kneel in prayer this morning to open the day seeking the guidance of the Lord. If you are one of those that did not, I would encourage you to commit in your heart to approach God in prayer at the beginning of every new day. Our Father in Heaven is eager to hear from you.

The scriptures are full of the admonition to pray. In 3 Nephi 18:15–21, the Lord repeats the instruction six times that we must pray. If we do not, He warns, we run the risk of being "tempted by the devil, [and] led away captive by him" (v. 15). In what ways does the adversary do this? One way is through discouragement, tempting us to abandon hope. He might say to us that we are not smart enough or talented enough to achieve our goals. He could begin to fire a few darts that lead us to say, "I'm too discouraged tonight. I'm not going to pray—what's the point?" Thus we start letting basic things slip that could keep us close to the Lord and help us to use our full potential. Then discouragement builds further discouragement.

Prayer has great power to chase away discouragement if you approach it humbly. It will cause you to repent. It will cause you to draw closer to the Lord. It will invite the hope of the Spirit into your life. I bear witness that there is great power in prayer. Humble yourselves before the Lord and pray to Him every day so that He has more opportunities to communicate His love and grace to you. Make it a sacred conversation with Heavenly Father, the God of the universe. Make it personal and listen carefully.

READ THE SCRIPTURES

It is not a new suggestion to read the scriptures every day—this basic practice keeps us tethered to the Lord. All the prophets since the Restoration of the gospel have instructed us to read the scriptures daily. I promise that if you spend even a few minutes studying each day, the Lord will speak to you through those scriptures. His message of comfort and hope will reach through any darkness you face. If we open our eyes of understanding and are ready to be taught by the Spirit, we will hear and we will learn.

Great strength will come out of personal, prayerful scripture study. When you are discouraged, go to the scriptures, and the Spirit will guide you to find the balm of Gilead. Light will enter your mind and the Spirit of the Lord will help you to find answers to your questions. Memorize some verses that are meaningful to you so that you always have them ready in times of despair. Establish a sacred storehouse of memory filled with precious scriptural nuggets. This is one of the ways we accept the Savior's loving admonition found in Doctrine and Covenants 6:36: "Look unto me in every thought; doubt not, fear not."

SERVE OTHERS

You might remember the wonderful lesson President Gordon B. Hinckley shared from a letter his father wrote him during his mission. When then-Elder Hinckley was discouraged and wondered if he was of any service to anyone, his father wrote to him, "Forget yourself and go to work."[1] We could add, "Forget yourself, go to work, and serve someone else." If you do this, discouragement will surely be gone. The more we try to help and serve others, the more we forget about our own challenges and problems.

If you see someone who is discouraged, or someone who is sitting alone in need of cheer, have the courage to ask how they are doing or sit with them. Maybe all they need is a smile. Maybe it is saying a silent prayer for them. Whatever the manner of reaching out to someone in need, you will feel an increase of hope and light in your own life as you follow the Savior's example of ministering to the one.

If you are presently struggling with a difficult burden, please do not hesitate to ask your bishop or your Relief Society president or your ministers for a blessing or prayers on your behalf. I bear witness that if you will do these simple things, the Spirit of the Lord will abide with you and your discouragement will flee.

As in all things, we can look to Jesus Christ as an example. How did Jesus spend His time? He spent it with the poor, the needy, the downcast, the downtrodden, even those in deep trouble. He served them and gave them hope. And that is how we can help each other and strengthen ourselves and one another to find hope and to turn continually to the Lord.

In her later years, my mother-in-law, Carmen Reich, a wonderful lady who had accepted the gospel message and joined the Church as a young mother, had to move into a nursing home. She was an eloquent speaker and could write like a poet. Toward the end of her life, she didn't say very much—just a few words here and there, with a beautiful smile that lightened up our lives. We knew that she appreciated very much when we sat with her holding her hand, helping her to eat, and sharing our feelings with her. Just being close to her and feeling the love and the sacred spirit that was in her room, we always felt blessed beyond measure and found our own hearts and burdens lightened because of her presence.

The Master said, "Whosoever will save his life shall lose it: and whosoever will lose his life for my sake shall find it" (Matthew 16:25). We can lose our lives in helping and serving others, and in so doing, we will find the hope and joy of the Savior.

YOU ARE BETTER THAN YOU THINK YOU ARE

Even the most successful among us need to be reminded of our worth from time to time. Consider, for example, Fred Astaire—the iconic actor, dancer, and singer. He starred in dozens of Broadway and Hollywood shows. When the American Film Institute ranked the top twenty-five male film legends of all time, Fred Astaire was number five on the list.[2]

However, when Mr. Astaire first auditioned for roles in Hollywood, he was considered quite ordinary. In fact, in one of his early auditions, they said of him: "Can't act. Can't sing. Balding. Can dance a little."[3] Those close to Fred Astaire knew that he was tormented with feelings of inadequacy. Even so, through persistence and hard work, he developed his abilities and became known for his "elegance, grace, originality, and precision."[4]

He was not the only one who struggled with self-doubt or endured criticism.

Walt Disney was fired from a newspaper because "he lacked imagination and had no good ideas."[5]

Some time ago, one of Vincent van Gogh's paintings sold for more than 15 million dollars.[6] However, during his lifetime, Vincent van Gogh sold only a very few paintings—and most of them went to family and close friends.[7]

We find many similar examples in the Old Testament. The reluctant warrior and hero Gideon thought of himself as an ordinary farmer. He said, "My family is poor in Manasseh, and I am the least in my father's house" (Judges 6:15). But an angel of God called Gideon a "mighty man of valour" and told him that with the Lord's help, he would liberate his people from the oppressive yoke of a conquering nation (Judges 6:12).

Gideon wasn't so sure about that. "Wherewith shall I save Israel?" he wondered (Judges 6:15). And yet the Lord took that self-doubting, humble farmer and turned him into a national hero—someone whose faith still inspires us today, more than three thousand years later (see Judges 6–7).

That seems to be the Lord's way, throughout history. He has always used the small and weak things of the world to bring about His glorious purposes (see Alma 26:12; 37:6).

Jeremiah believed he was too young to be a prophet (see Jeremiah 1:6–7).

Moses doubted himself because he was "slow of speech" (Exodus 4:10).

Enoch felt inadequate to preach repentance because, in his words, "all the people hate me" (Moses 6:31).

The Lord often accomplishes the most with those who feel the least accomplished.

He took a young shepherd and made him mighty in slaying an imposing giant and leading a fledgling nation into greatness (see 1 Samuel 17).

He took a young priest serving a wicked king and made him the leader of a band of refugee believers. Later, God called this same man to lead the entire church of the Nephite nation (see Mosiah 17–18; 23–27).

In our dispensation, God took a young, unschooled farm boy and mentored him until he became the great latter-day prophet who began "a marvelous work and a wonder" that is now rolling forth unto every nation of the world (2 Nephi 27:26; see also Isaiah 29:14).

Perhaps, at times, we see ourselves as a little less than we are. Unworthy. Untalented. Nothing special. Lacking the heart, mind, resources, charisma, or stature to be of much use to God. You say you're not perfect? You're not good enough? Well, welcome to the club! You may be just the person God is looking for.

Listen to what the Apostle Paul wrote to the Saints in Corinth two thousand years ago and see if his words do not speak to you today. They certainly speak to me. Paul said: "Brothers and sisters, think of what you were when you were called. Not many of you were wise by human standards; not many were influential; not many were of noble birth. But God chose the foolish things of the world to shame the wise. . . . God chose the lowly things of this world and the despised things . . . so that no one may boast before him" (1 Corinthians 1:26–29, New International Version).

The Lord chooses the humble and meek—partly *because* they are humble and meek. In this way, there is never a question regarding the reason for their success. These wonderful, ordinary people accomplish great things not because of who *they* are *but because of who God is!*

For "what is impossible with man is possible with God" (Luke 18:27, NIV; see also Mark 10:27). God will take your talents and abilities and multiply them—even though they may seem as scarce as a few loaves and fishes. If you trust Him and are faithful, He will magnify your words and actions and use them to bless and minister to multitudes! (see John 6:8–13).

God does not need people who are flawless. He seeks those who will offer their "heart and a willing mind," and He will make them "perfect in Christ" (Doctrine and Covenants 64:34, see also verses 31–33; Moroni 10:32–33).

I bear testimony that these things are true. I pray that we may turn to God, that we will address Him in our prayers and listen to Him in our scriptures. I pray that we will act upon the teachings of the Spirit by serving others and that we will help others to be joyful at all times by having a song and hymn of the righteous in our heart. Let us love God, our Heavenly Father, and His Son, Jesus Christ, and love our neighbor by helping and serving one another. In this, we will overcome discouragement and feel the Lord's grace settling into our lives.

Conclusion

A HIGHER JOY

I t's hard to believe it was only 120 years ago when Wilbur and Orville Wright first lifted off and flew over the sands of Kitty Hawk, North Carolina. Four short flights on that December day changed the world and opened the door to one of the greatest inventions in history.

Flying was risky in those early days. The brothers knew this. And so did their father, Milton. In fact, he was so terrified of losing both of his sons in a flying accident that they promised him they would never fly together. And they never did—with one exception. Seven years after that historic day at Kitty Hawk, Milton Wright finally gave his consent and watched as Wilbur and Orville flew together for the first time. After landing, Orville convinced his father to take his first and only flight and to see for himself what it was like.

As the plane lifted from the ground, the eighty-two-year-old Milton got so caught up in the exhilaration of flight that all fear left him. Orville rejoiced as his father shouted with delight, "Higher, Orville, higher!"[1]

This was a man after my own heart!

Perhaps the reason I speak about aviation occasionally is that I know something of what the Wrights felt. I too have "slipped the surly bonds of Earth and danced the skies on laughter-silvered wings."[2] The Wright brothers' first flight, which happened a mere thirty-seven years before my birth, opened doors of adventure, wonder, and pure joy into my life.

And yet, as amazing as that joy is, there is an even higher kind of joy. In the spirit of Milton Wright's delighted cry, "Higher, Orville, higher," I would like to discuss this higher joy—where it comes from, how it enters our hearts, and how we can experience it in greater measure.

THE WHOLE AIM OF HUMAN EXISTENCE

It probably goes without saying that everyone wants to be happy. Twenty-four hundred years ago, Aristotle observed that happiness is the one thing all humans desire most. In his treatise Nicomachean Ethics, he taught that the greatest good in life is the thing we pursue as an end itself (as opposed to those things we pursue that are a means to some other end). Happiness, above all else, is just such a thing. "We always desire happiness for its own sake," he said, "and never as a means to something else."[3] Nevertheless, it also goes without saying that not everyone is happy. Sadly, it seems that for many people, happiness is hard to find.[4]

Why is that? If happiness is the one thing we humans desire most, why are we so unsuccessful at finding it? To paraphrase a country song, maybe we've been looking for joy in all the wrong places.[5]

Before we consider how to find joy, allow me to acknowledge that depression and other difficult mental and emotional challenges are real, and the answer is not simply "Try to be happier." I do not want to diminish or trivialize mental health issues. If you face such challenges, I mourn with you, and I stand beside you. For some people, finding joy may include seeking help from trained mental health professionals who devote their lives to practicing their very important art. We should be thankful for such help.

Life is not an endless sequence of emotional highs. "For it must needs be, that there is an opposition in all things" (2 Nephi 2:11). And if God Himself weeps, as the scriptures affirm He does, then of course you and I will weep as well (see John 11:35; Moses 7:28–37). Feeling sad is not a sign of failure. In this life, at least, joy and sorrow are inseparable companions (see 2 Nephi 2:11). Like all of you, I have felt my share of disappointment, sorrow, sadness, and remorse.

However, I have also experienced for myself the glorious dawn that fills the soul with joy so profound that it can scarcely be kept in. I have discovered for myself that this peaceful confidence comes from following the Savior and walking in His Way.

The peace He gives us is not like what the world gives (see John 14:27). It's better. It's higher and holier. Jesus said, "I am come that they might have life, and that they might have it more abundantly" (John 10:10).

The gospel of Jesus Christ is truly the "good news of great joy"! (Luke 2:10, New Revised Standard Version). It is a message of matchless hope! A message of yoke-bearing and burden-lifting (see Matthew 11:28–30). Of light-gathering. Of heavenly favor, higher understanding, holier covenants, eternal security, and everlasting glory!

Joy is the very purpose of God's plan for His children. It's what you were created for—"that [you] might have joy"! (2 Nephi 2:25). You were built for this!

Our Father in Heaven has not hidden the path to happiness. It is not a secret. It is available to all!

If you have any concerns about whether or not your Father in Heaven will accept you and allow you to receive His joy, I invite you to prayerfully return to Christ's parable of the prodigal son that we reviewed earlier and read it again (see Luke 15:11–32). In that parable, we learn how our Heavenly Father feels about His children and how He awaits and celebrates our return after we have strayed from Him. From the moment we "come to ourselves" (see verse 17) and begin the journey home, He will see us, for He stands watching and waiting. And what is He waiting for? For us! As we draw near to Him, He will celebrate our return and call us His child.

His welcoming embrace is promised to those who walk the path of discipleship, follow the teachings and example of the Savior, keep His commandments, and honor covenants they make with God. What a remarkable promise!

GOD HAS SOMETHING MORE TO OFFER

We all know people who say that they don't need God to be happy, or that they are happy enough without religion. I acknowledge and respect these feelings. Our beloved Father in Heaven wants all His children to have as much happiness as possible, so He has filled this world with beautiful, wholesome pleasures and delights, "both to please the eye and to gladden the heart" (Doctrine and Covenants 59:18). This revelation also explains, "It pleaseth God that he hath given all these things unto man; for unto this end were they made" (verse 20). For me, flying brought great happiness. Others find it in music, in art, in hobbies, or in nature.

By inviting everyone and sharing the Savior's good news of great joy, we do not discount any of these sources of joy. We're simply saying that God has something more to give. A higher and more profound joy—a joy that transcends anything this world offers. It is a joy that endures heartbreak, penetrates sorrow, and diminishes loneliness.

Worldly happiness, by contrast, does not last. It cannot. It is the nature of all earthly things to grow old, decay, wear out, or become stale. But godly joy is eternal, because God is eternal. Jesus Christ came to lift us out of the temporal and replace corruption with incorruption. Only He has that power, and only His joy is perpetual.

If you feel there could be more of this kind of joy in your life, I invite you to embark on the journey of following Jesus Christ and His Way. Living in hope, grace, and joy is a journey of a lifetime—and beyond. Please let me review a few beginning steps on this worthy journey of discovering pure joy.

DRAW NEAR UNTO GOD

To those who draw near to God, He gives this grand promise: "I will draw near unto you" (Doctrine and Covenants 88:63; see also James 4:8). Do you remember the woman in the New Testament who endured a bleeding illness for twelve years? (see Mark 5:24–34). She had spent all she had on physicians, but things only grew worse. She had heard of Jesus; His power to heal was well known. But could He heal her? And how could she even get near Him? Her sickness made her "unclean" according to the law of Moses, and therefore she was required to stay away from others.

Approaching Him openly and asking for healing seemed out of the question.

Still, she thought, "If I may touch but his clothes, I shall be whole" (Mark 5:28).

At last, her faith overcame her fear. She braved the censure of others and pressed toward the Savior.

Finally, she was within reach. She extended her hand.

And she was healed.

Aren't we all somewhat like this woman?

There may be many reasons why we hesitate to draw near to the Savior. We may face ridicule or condemnation by others. In our pride, we may dismiss the possibility of something so simple being of so much value. We may think that our condition somehow disqualifies us from His healing—that the distance is too great or our sins too many.

Like this woman, I have learned that if we draw near to God and reach out to touch Him, we can indeed find grace, healing, peace, and joy. Jesus taught, "Seek, and ye shall find" (Matthew 7:7). I believe this simple phrase is not only a spiritual promise; it is a statement of fact. If we seek reasons to be angry, to doubt, to be bitter or alone, we will find them too. However, if we seek joy—if we look for reasons to rejoice and to happily follow the Savior, we will find them. We rarely find something we are not looking for.

Are you looking for joy?

Seek, and ye shall find.

BEAR ONE ANOTHER'S BURDENS

By bearing each other's burdens, we "fulfil the law of Christ" (Galatians 6:2; see also Mosiah 18:8). Jesus taught, "It is more blessed to give than to receive" (Acts 20:35). Can it be that in our search for joy, the best way to find it is to bring joy to others? My friends, you know and I know this is true! Joy is like a barrel of flour or a jar of oil that will never run out (see 1 Kings 17:8–16). True joy multiplies when it is shared.

It doesn't require something grand or complicated.

We can do simple things.

Like praying for someone with all our heart.

Giving a sincere compliment.

Helping someone feel welcome, respected, valued, and loved.

Sharing a favorite scripture and what it means to us.

Or even just by listening.

"When ye are in the service of your fellow beings ye are only in the service of your God," and God will repay your kindness generously (Mosiah 2:17). In his Epistle to the Romans, Paul states that God "will render to every man according to his deeds: to them who by patient continuance in well doing seek for glory and honour and immortality, eternal life: . . . glory, honour, and peace, to every man that worketh good" (Romans 2:6–7, 10). The joy you give to others will return to you in "good measure, pressed down, and shaken together, and running over" (Luke 6:38). Our very salvation and eternal happiness may depend on our compassion and kindness to others (see Matthew 25:31–46).

"WHAT SHALL WE DO THEN?" (LUKE 3:10)

During the coming days, weeks, and months, may I invite you to:

- Spend time in a sincere, full-hearted effort to draw near to God.
- Seek diligently for everyday moments of hope, grace, peace, and joy.
- Bring joy to others around you.

My dear brothers and sisters, dear friends, as you search the word of God for a deeper understanding of God's eternal plan, accept these invitations, and strive to walk in His way, you will experience "the peace of God, which passeth all understanding," even in the midst of sorrows (Philippians 4:7). You will feel a greater measure of God's unsurpassable love swelling within your heart. The grace of Jesus Christ will settle into your soul, offering you hope to keep pressing forward even when it seems impossible. The dawn of celestial light will penetrate the shadows of your trials, and you will begin to taste the unspeakable glories and wonders of the unseen, perfect, heavenly sphere. You will feel your spirit lifting away from the gravity of this world.

And like good Milton Wright, perhaps you will raise your voice in rejoicing and shout, "Higher, Father, higher!"

NOTES

INTRODUCTION

1. "The 20 Richest People of All Time," April 25, 2017, msn.com.

CHAPTER 1: THE INFINITE POWER OF HOPE

1. See, for example, 1 Corinthians 13:13; Alma 7:24; Ether 12:28; Moroni 7:1; 8:14; 10:20–21; Doctrine and Covenants 4:5; 6:19; 12:8; 18:19.
2. Albert Camus, in John Bartlett, comp., *Familiar Quotations*, 17th ed. (2002), 790.

CHAPTER 2: THE GIFT OF GRACE

1. In saying "we have all sinned," I refer to all who possess a basic understanding of good and evil and who reach the age of accountability in mortality. We know from scripture that little children are not capable of committing sin (see Moroni 8:8; Doctrine and Covenants 137:10).
2. See Brigham Young, "Discourse," February 3, 1867, *Deseret News*, March 13, 1867.
3. Stephen E. Robinson, *Believing Christ* (Salt Lake City: Deseret Book, 1992), 92;

see also Robert L. Millet and Gerald R. McDermott, *Claiming Christ: A Mormon-Evangelical Debate* (Grand Rapids, MI: Brazos Press, 2007), 188.

4. M. Russell Ballard, "That We May Know," BYU–Hawaii devotional, January 25, 2001, https://speeches.byuh.edu/devotionals/that-we-might-know; emphasis added.

5. Quentin L. Cook, "Be True to God and His Work," *Liahona*, November 2022.

6. Russell M. Nelson, "We Can Do Better and Be Better," *Ensign*, May 2019.

CHAPTER 3: PRODIGALS ALL

1. By Jewish law and tradition, the older of two sons was entitled to a two-thirds portion of the father's inheritance. The younger son, therefore, was entitled to a one-third portion (see Deuteronomy 21:17).

2. Elder Neal A. Maxwell taught: "Of course, it is better if we are humbled 'because of the word' rather than being [humbled] by circumstances, yet the latter may do! (see Alma 32:13–14). Famine can induce spiritual hunger" ("The Tugs and Pulls of the World," *Ensign*, November 2000).

3. Jeffrey R. Holland, "The Laborers in the Vineyard," *Ensign*, May 2012.

CHAPTER 4: LIVING IN GRACE AND HOPE

1. Matthew 6:33, footnote a.

2. Russell M. Nelson, *From Heart to Heart: An Autobiography* (1979), 114.

3. Russell M. Nelson, "Welcome Message," *Liahona*, May 2021.

4. Spencer W. Kimball, *The Miracle of Forgiveness* (Salt Lake City: Deseret Book, 1976), 363, 368.

CHAPTER 5: LOVING GOD AND OUR NEIGHBORS

1. Camille N. Johnson, "Lessons Learned in Inviting Christ to Author My Story," BYU Women's Conference address, May 3, 2024.

2. See Errol Morris, "The Anosognosic's Dilemma: Something's Wrong but You'll Never Know What It Is," *New York Times*, June 20, 2010; opinionator.blogs.nytimes.com/2010/06/20/the-anosognosics-dilemma-1.

3. See Justin Kruger and David Dunning, "Unskilled and Unaware of It: How Difficulties in Recognizing One's Own Incompetence Lead to Inflated Self-Assessments," *Journal of Personality and Social Psychology*, Dec. 1999, 1121–34.

4. See Marshall Goldsmith, *What Got You Here Won't Get You There* (2007), chapter 3.

5. See Exodus 14:13–14; Deuteronomy 3:21–22; Psalm 20:6; 34:17; Proverbs 20:22.

6. Reyna I. Aburto, "Thru Cloud and Sunshine, Lord, Abide with Me!," *Ensign*, November 2019.

CHAPTER 6: OVERCOMING DISCOURAGEMENT

1. Gordon B. Hinckley, "Taking the Gospel to Britain: A Declaration of Vision, Faith, Courage, and Truth," *Ensign*, July 1987.

2. See "AFI's 100 Years . . . 100 Stars: The 50 Greatest American Screen Legends," lists, American Film Institute, https://www.afi.com/afis-100-years-100-stars.

3. In John E. Mueller, *Astaire Dancing: The Musical Films* (London: Hamish Hamilton, 1986), 7, note 3; see also Wikipedia, s.v. "Fred Astaire."

4. Wikipedia, s.v. "Fred Astaire."

5. Colleen Kane, "Successes That Almost Weren't," Slideshows, CNBC, 18 November 2011, cnbc.com/2011/11/18/Successes-That-Almost-Werent.html; quoted in Rachel Gillett, "How Walt Disney, Oprah Winfrey, and 19 Other Successful People Rebounded After Getting Fired," *Inc.,* 7 October 2015, inc.com/business-insider/21-successful-people-who-rebounded-after-getting-fired.html.

6. See Rob Picheta and Chloe Adams, "Unseen Vincent van Gogh Painting of Paris Sells for $15.4M," Style, CNN, 29 March 2021, cnn.com/style/article/van-gogh-paris-painting-public-display-scli-intl/index.html.

7. See "How Many Paintings Did Vincent Sell During His Lifetime?" Vincent van Gogh FAQs, Van Gogh Museum, vangoghmuseum.nl/en/art-and-stories/vincent-van-gogh-faq/how-many-paintings-did-vincent-sell-during-his-lifetime.

CONCLUSION: A HIGHER JOY

1. See Christopher Klein, "10 Things You May Not Know about the Wright Brothers," History, Mar. 28, 2023, history.com.

2. Magee, "High Flight."

3. The Nicomachean Ethics of Aristotle, trans. J. E. C. Weldon (1902), 13–14.

4. See Harry Enten, "American Happiness Hits Record Lows," CNN, Feb. 2, 2022, cnn.com; Tamara Lush, "Poll: Americans Are the Unhappiest They've Been in 50 Years," Associated Press, June 16, 2020, apnews.com; "The Great Gloom: In 2023, Employees Are Unhappier Than Ever. Why?" BambooHR, bamboohr.com.

5. See Wanda Mallette, Patti Ryan, and Bob Morrison, "Lookin' for Love (in All the Wrong Places)" (1980).

ABOUT THE AUTHOR

ELDER DIETER F. UCHTDORF was called as Second Counselor in the First Presidency of The Church of Jesus Christ of Latter-day Saints on February 3, 2008. He served in that position until January 2018. He has served as a General Authority since April 1994. Prior to his calling as a General Authority, Elder Uchtdorf was the senior vice president of flight operations and chief pilot of Lufthansa German Airlines. Elder Uchtdorf was born in 1940 in what is now the Czech Republic. He grew up in Zwickau, Germany, where his family joined the Church in 1947. He and his wife, Harriet Reich Uchtdorf, are the parents of two children and have six grandchildren and six great-grandchildren.